"*Thriving in the City* is an outstar[...] [...]p.ov.ucs valuable insights into the issues and options faced by those who seek to live meaningfully among the urban poor as agents for transformation. It is a must-read for those whom God is calling to live among the urban poor and those wanting to support others in this path."

- *Kevin Walton, Vice-President, Thai Peace Foundation*

"While incarnational strategies in urban poor communities are not new, every practitioner knows there is hardly ever any discussion of those issues that affect sustainability—until now. Smith has contributed something of immense value, which brims with authentic experience and insight wrought from the pain and beauty of his Botocan community."

- *Randy White, Author of* Encounter God in the City

"This book covers the waterfront on incarnational ministry to a depth I have not seen in any other book. It works with this theme theologically, biblically, methodologically, attitudinally, and practically. And the reason it treats the subject so thoroughly is because Aaron and Ema Smith live it."

- *Robert C. Linthicum, Founding Director of World Vision's Urban Advance, Pastor of Urban Churches, and Community Organizer*

"This is an insightful and reflective work—a rich, thoughtful reflection on the decisions facing those who would live among the people they minister to—particularly among the poor. It is powerful in story-telling and brings clarity to the base truths we hope to live out. May we be found faithful in them."

- *Kevin Blue, Author of* Practical Justice

"This is a powerful read. It calls growing ministers to draw from proven principles in solidarity with the poor, cross-cultural living, and church planting. But just as importantly, readers will be inspired Aaron's own testimony of a life poured out for God's cause. If you are considering ministry of presence and advocacy for social justice, and if you believe in the central role of the church in social transformation, I would highly recommend this book."

— *Maripaz Batik, Church Planting Team Leader;*
Adjunct Professor, Asian Theological Seminary

"*Thriving in the City* is a gift to the emerging movement serving the urban poor. Beginning with one of the most thoughtful explorations on what it means to be incarnational, Smith takes us on a journey through his experiences living in desperately poor communities. He has constructed a practical guide for those seeking to enflesh the gospel while living alongside our neighbors on the margins of the empire. For those living or planning to live among the urban poor, whether in the high poverty neighborhoods of the West or the favelas and barrios of the Majority World, consider this book a part of your weaponry."

— *Scott Bessenecker, Associate Director of Missions,*
InterVarsity Christian Fellowship

"*Thriving in the City* is one of the finest books on incarnational ministry that I've read. The power behind Aaron Smith's theological reflection comes from the fact that he has lived and raised a family in squatter communities for many years. His stories and insights are both practical and inspirational, urging us all to greater faithfulness to Jesus' call.

— *Lisa Engdahl, General Director, Servant Partners*

THRIVING
IN THE CITY

THRIVING
IN THE CITY

A GUIDE FOR SUSTAINABLE INCARNATIONAL MINISTRY AMONG THE URBAN POOR

T. AARON SMITH
foreword by Viv Grigg

SERVANT PARTNERS PRESS

CONTENTS

FOREWORD

IT'S A FASCINATING CONCEPT, this following Jesus among the poor. Incarnation. Solidarity. Identification. It's so simple: we follow after Jesus, in the lineage of Paul to St. Francis of Assisi to St. Francis Xavier to the Methodist circuit riders to the million Pentecostal slum pastors of today across the world's 6,600 mostly new slum cities.

Yet this life of simplicity is so complex to master. And that is where a practical book on the steps and processes of moving from wealth to poverty becomes critical. A stream of 50,000 workers have moved to the world's slums in these last ten years, and the field of urban poor missiology has exploded as more and more schools around the globe offer MAs in Transformational Urban Leadership. Recently, as I was designing a course on Urban Poor Spirituality to train my university's next class of enthusiastic DUPPies (Downwardly Mobile Professionals), I wondered where I could find a comprehensive, easy-to-read, and practical text to help my students to thrive in their new cities. As I began to read Aaron's book, I knew that I had found it.

In Manila, standing in the long tradition of poor community pastors and wandering preachers among the poor, T. Aaron Smith and his wife Ema faithfully continue to dwell, to minister, and to train those who would follow. Ever the consummate teacher, Aaron dissects the details of a lifestyle and calling conversationally, humorously, and in a biblically reflective manner. Over a decade of ministry gives him credibility. I have visited his church and watched it blossom and persist with my own eyes. Raising a family and forming a church indicate both an integrity of being and fruitfulness, for the call is primarily to go preach and bear fruit, and that as rapidly as we can. But the manner, the style, the foundation is to be in the same way that the Father sent our Lord—and he came as poor to the poor. He came preaching to the poor, and the poor heard him gladly for he spoke as one of them with their stories, their humor, their perspectives—the incarnate one, forming the incarnate movements of believers among the poor.

It's good to learn from Aaron how to follow this Jesus. I would encourage all who are seeking to follow this Jesus into our world's slums to engage with this book along their journey.

Viv Grigg
Wandering servant of urban poor workers
International Director, Urban
Leadership Foundation
Catalyst, MA in Transformational Urban
Leadership in seven seminaries globally
Assoc Prof, Urban Missions, MATUL,
Azusa Pacific Seminary

NOVEMBER 2015

INTRODUCTION

"TRAIN!" A WOMAN SHOUTED, warning her neighbors to move off the railroad tracks. This was not the normal passenger train that usually sped down the tracks next to Balic-Balic. It moved about as fast as a casual walk and towed only one flatbed railroad car, which carried dozens of police officers wearing full-body armor and assault rifles. These police officers were there to maintain peace and order, so to speak, while homes along the train tracks were razed. The railroad communities south of us had already disappeared into an ever-approaching dust cloud, and their arrival signaled that it was our turn to be scattered.

For a full week, the sound of sledgehammers breaking up concrete resounded throughout the community. The first squatter home I had ever slept in was destroyed. The church where I had delivered my first sermon and led countless Bible studies was turned into a pile of broken cinder blocks. Every home and building in the community was turned to rubble. Seven years later, the sounds floating out of construction sites still make me flinch.

When I first moved into a squatter community, I knew that the physical discomforts would be stressful. Aspects of urban poor life such as carrying water in buckets, sleeping on the floor, and having cockroaches as roommates were difficult, but manageable. But the emotional pain of seeing our home, church, and community deliberately destroyed made my wife and I want to quit altogether.

It's no wonder that burnout is so common among those who work with the poor. Urban ministry leader David Claerbaut writes, "Among urban workers in general, whether they are teachers, pastors, social workers, or any other professionals who work regularly with problem-plagued people, the average length of service is not much more than four years."[1] By 2008, I was wondering whether my family's decade among the urban poor would be quietly folded into the upper end of that statistic.

As I stood at this violent crossroads, I began to wonder at the process of learning to thrive in the midst of urban poverty. Living incarnationally,[2] or ministering through meaningful, engaged presence, in the midst of the extremes of pain and joy found in the world's slums was not easy, but it was remarkably possible. Though I had seen many incarnational leaders come and go, I knew that there were also many who had stayed, and in fact had gone on to build full and rich lives and ministries among the urban poor. Movement leader Viv Grigg writes of incarnational leaders, "Somewhere, ten to fifteen years into their ministries, they often entered into a deeper life, a new empowering of the Spirit of God."[3] But how did they get there? How could Ema and I last—how could anyone last—for the decades required to see real internal fruit and external transformation?

A few years later, I was blessed to have the opportunity to pursue my Doctorate of Ministry in Transformational Leadership for the Global City at Bakke Graduate University, where I delved deeply into these questions. My doctoral dissertation opened the door for me to survey 100 of my fellow urban ministers, both current and former. I conducted dozens of follow-up interviews and multiple focus groups. We talked about what worked and what didn't, how they found the strength to stay and why they didn't, and what advice they might have for those just beginning their careers among the urban poor. As a follow-up to my studies, I joined their experience with my own to form what became an early version of this book.[4] This heavily revised edition more fully integrates their voices to provide insight for those who long to stay.

But the origin of this book does not begin with a dissertation. It begins with a little boy listening to his grandmothers' stories.

My Story

People often ask me how I, a middle-class American, ended up living in a squatter community in Manila. Simply put, I was called to it. Everything in my spiritual life and circumstances began to point me here. But stepping into my calling was a long process, a process that might look very different from your own. I share it here so that you will have an understanding of my perspective.

I learned the importance of economic justice from an early age. My parents had their share of financial struggles, so I was never allowed to believe that I was somehow better than people in poverty. I also remember listening to my grandparents' stories of justice and concern for the poor. Grandma Lotz grew up as the daughter of a small town doctor. During the Great Depression, she never knew the intense poverty that others faced, but she always acted with prayerful compassion toward them. Even as a frail elderly woman, her prayers before meals included the hungry. Grandma Smith also had a compassionate heart and a deep desire for justice. She often told the story of how, in the 1930s, she broke up with her high school sweetheart because he told her not to sit next to an African American girl on the school bus. She sat next to that girl for the rest of the school year. Hearing these stories as a young child instilled in me a heart for justice and human dignity.

For most of my adolescence, my compassion for the oppressed was not strong enough to result in any kind of meaningful action. My friends and I complained about injustice, but we did not change our lifestyle because of it. I still aspired to live the American dream, securing a good job that would allow me to buy a nice house, a car, and a sense of safety and status.

It wasn't until college that God began to work on changing my heart and calling me to the urban poor. It really began with getting involved in InterVarsity Christian Fellowship at my university. I joined a small group Bible study and met weekly with Brian, a godly student who helped me to grow in Christ and to shape the direction of my future toward something bigger than personal ambition.

Then, in the process of researching an essay during my junior year, I went to pick up a video related to agricultural economics from the library. I must have written the wrong call number down, because the video given to me was about rural squatters in Brazil. Though it had nothing to do with the topic of my paper, I was completely drawn to the video's vivid depictions of the raw poverty in that community. I left the library unable to focus on my paper. My mind was occupied by the plight of the poor.

At an InterVarsity large group meeting later that month, several students presented on their recent exposure trips and short-term missions. One student shared about an annual six-week trip to a squatter community in Manila. When I spoke to her afterward, she gave me a copy of Viv Grigg's book, *Companion to the Poor*. The more I read and learned, the more I became intrigued with the idea of living in an urban slum, teaching the Bible, and working for community transformation.

The following round of exposure trips took place right before my senior year, and I joined the team that would go to Manila for six weeks. However, that particular year, we were sent to a middle-class student ministry in the countryside. The disappointment I felt confirmed my own strong drive to live among the poor, as did our week spent in Manila doing culture and language study before beginning our student ministry. This trip was also significant in that we were hosted by the professor who would soon encourage me to come to study at Asian Theological Seminary in Manila. I saw this as my fast track ticket to living among the squatters in that city.

The year that followed was spent in preparation for life and ministry among the urban poor. I read every book I could get my hands on, and I tried to form meaningful connections with the homeless and very poor around my own college community. After graduation, I worked for six months in order to save up for seminary and my plane ticket. The concept of fundraising had never occurred to me. Finally, on a cold rainy day in November of 1997, I boarded a plane for Manila.

My first week was extremely challenging. I spoke very little Tagalog, I didn't know anybody, and I was deliriously tired from the jet lag. A professor at ATS helped me to find a place to live, but it wasn't in a squatter community. As that was one of the main reasons I went to Manila, I began to wonder if there was any point to this bewildering adventure. I decided I would tell the professor I had made a mistake, change my ticket, and return home.

But God would not let me. That's the only way to describe it! The whole next day, I kept opening my mouth to speak, but no words came out. Meanwhile, my professor's wife was busily helping me set up a bank account and make purchases for the school year. I was running out of time; the longer I waited, the harder it would be to leave Manila. I said to myself, "Okay, I am going to tell her on the count of three. One, two, three." But the words refused to come. That evening, I finally prayed, "All right, God, you have showed me this is where you want me. I am going to stay."

The wrong video, the mission presentation, receiving *Companion to the Poor*, meeting a professor from Asian Theological Seminary, and miraculously not being able to talk: all of these events helped me to persevere during the years when I really wanted to leave the urban poor for something easier. This is the vital importance of our origin stories, and our overall sense of continued calling.

After two months in Manila, I met the pastor from Balic-Balic Christian Church. He invited me to help with their youth service, an opportunity which I eagerly accepted. I commuted to the church on Saturday mornings and would stay with the pastor and his mother until Monday morning. I relished this time to learn the culture and build relationships with people in the church.

At the end of the school year, I went back to the US to work sixty-hour weeks in a construction job all summer. I could save about $3,000 in those two months, giving me about $1,000 for a round trip plane ticket, $1,000 for two semesters of tuition, $150 for my visa, and $85 each month to pay for all of my living expenses. Many urban poor families lived on $85 a month, so I figured I should too.

I finally moved into Balic-Balic during my second year, when the pastor accepted the call to serve in another church. I took his old house and continued ministering with the small group of committed followers of Jesus in Balic-Balic Christian Church (BBCC). We would often gather together to sing, share about God's goodness, and pray.

That first year living in Balic-Balic was an overwhelming one, and I almost burned myself out. However, as I was committed to both the community and my schooling, I decided to stay. Over time, I learned about my own limits and begin to see real fruit as God worked through our community. This ministry would also introduce me to Ema, the local leader who would soon become my wife and ministry partner. After I graduated from ATS, we returned to the US. We quickly began looking for an organization that would provide a support structure so that we could return to Balic-Balic as full-time ministers.

I found Servant Partners by accident. I first thought I was applying to SERVANTS (Servants to Asia's Urban Poor), a different organization with a similar focus. I didn't realize my mistake until I was well into the application process, but by then I had learned more about Servant Partners and decided it might just be the right organization for Ema and me. Servant Partners has proven to be a great fit for us. They provide the right balance of site freedom, as well as support and guidance from the larger organization. It took almost two years to find Servant Partners, raise support, and then complete our training, but we returned to Balic-Balic as Servant Partners staff as soon as we could. We remained there until the community was destroyed in 2008.

The recent birth of our son, Zach, made it especially tempting to leave urban poor ministry at that point, but we prayerfully discerned that we were to continue ministering as a family. We moved to Botocan, an urban poor community in a different part of Manila, where we have had the privilege of ministering as a growing family and seeing God work for the past seven years. In 2013, Ema and I welcomed our second healthy son, Ezra, into the community. Today, Ema, Zach, Ezra, and I are at home here. We see God moving every day, and we are committed to remaining here as long as we're called to do so.

About This Book

AUDIENCE. This book was mainly written for those who are exploring, preparing for, or practicing a life of incarnational ministry in urban settings. Many of the issues discussed are specific to the experience of career ministers who of relocate from middle-class communities in the West to the poorest communities of the Majority World. However, indigenous leaders, middle-class ministers, and those who work in student ministry have also benefited from the thoughts and questions put forth here. In general, this book is meant to equip incarnational leaders to make educated decisions regarding their lives and ministries, and to help them stay in their communities long enough to bring about true transformation.

Everyone's experience of incarnational ministry is different. What I struggle with may not bother others, and what does not bother me may be extremely difficult for others. This book is not a definitive how-to guide nor a manual for successful incarnational ministry. It was written to help you ask more thoughtful and helpful questions about your own ministry or potential ministry in places of poverty. As you read, pause to reflect and pray about applications to your own life.

RESEARCH. This book is a product of many incarnational leaders' generously shared experiences. Some of these were authors of wonderful books,[5] while many shared their wisdom with me more directly in the course of my dissertation research.

As I mentioned above, exactly 100 current and former incarnational leaders submitted detailed questionnaires about their experiences. Potential respondents were limited to those who relocated to an urban poor community for the purpose of ministry. The bulk of the participants were current and former incarnational workers from Servant Partners, SERVANTS, and Urban Neighbors of Hope (UNOH).

Over a dozen follow-up interviews refined and verified the questionnaire results and provided a rich store of true stories from the field. Two focus groups at Servant Partners staff conferences fostered rich discussions of some of the problems and solutions of living incarnationally. Finally, my research led me to more intentionally analyze my own continued experience in Manila as a form of participant observation. All of the stories shared here come from direct first-person accounts which came out of this research, though some names have been changed for anonymity.

THEOLOGY. This book is primarily practical rather than theological, but I aspire to root this book (and my own life) in Christian Scripture as it has been historically understood by the Church. My own denominational affiliation is Southern Baptist, but I am thankful for my broad exposure to other denominations, especially at my interdenominational Evangelical seminaries. This book was written to be relevant across affiliations. The Bible is quoted in the English Standard Version throughout the text.

ORGANIZATION. The two sections of this book loosely follow the phases of developing and sustaining this type of ministry. In Part I, "A Sustainable Understanding of Incarnational Ministry," I will lay out a vision for a holistic incarnational ministry that is built to last. Part II, "Practicing Sustainability in your Incarnational Ministry," is much more interactive. You will be asked to pause and reflect on three personal questions after each chapter section. If you are ministering incarnationally, considering doing so, or simply trying to live more incarnationally in your own context, I recommend thoroughly journaling your responses to more deeply reflect upon them, as well as discussing them with other readers.

At the back of this book, I've appended an article that discusses and defends the term *incarnational*, the research results from my dissertation, and a partial list of organizations that offer opportunities to immersively explore incarnational ministry. You will also find a glossary of terms and place names, a full bibliography that indicates suggestions for further reading, and an index of interviews that became part of this book, directly or indirectly. I pray that this book will be a useful resource for incarnational leaders of all types as they continue to walk faithfully in their journey with Jesus among the urban poor.

---

[1] David Clearbaut, *Urban Ministry in a New Millennium* (Waynesboro, GA: Authentic Media, 2005), 249-250.

[2] An explanation for the choice and use of the word *incarnational* is given in Appendix A, "Why 'Incarnational' Missions?" by Derek Engdahl.

[3] Viv Grigg, *Companion to the Poor: Christ in the Urban Slums* (Waynesboro, GA: Authentic Media, 2004), 123.

[4] Released in 2012 as *Living in the Neighborhood*, a pilot project of Servant Partners Press.

[5] See bibliography. Recommended reading is indicated in bold.

PART ONE:

A SUSTAINABLE UNDERSTANDING OF INCARNATIONAL MINISTRY

1

INCARNATION AND
THE CHRISTIAN FAITH

THE TERM *INCARNATIONAL MINISTRY* refers to *meaningful presence and engagement for transformation.* You might recognize that the word *incarnation* is based on the Latin word meaning "in the flesh". Incarnational ministry means not only being physically present ourselves, but also participating meaningfully in the transforming renewal of our communities so that God's presence will be more clearly visible there.

Though people of all beliefs might value living intentionally for the good of the community, Christ particularly calls and empowers his followers to live this way. The current popular buzz about incarnational ministry should not distract us from the deep scriptural and historical roots of this Christian calling. From God's transformative presence throughout Scripture, to Jeremiah's message that Israel should build, plant, and marry while exiled in Babylon,[6] to Christ's full participation in human life within a specific cultural context, our Scripture compels us to see the power in our own presence. We know that God calls us as he called the Israelites through Jeremiah, to "seek the *shalom* (the deep welfare, peace, and wholeness, both physical and spiritual) of the city where I have

15

sent you... and pray to the Lord on its behalf, for in its *shalom* you will find your *shalom*."[7] Our faith teaches us that our well-being is bound up with the well-being of our neighbors—with our participation in each other's well-being.

Clearly, living incarnationally can have a lot of different implications and applications. If you are called to teach in an upscale private school, you will have many opportunities to be present and engaged in your students' lives for the sake of Christ. If you are called to minister incarnationally among big business leaders or politicians, your meaningful presence might transform economic policies and legislation to more closely resemble God's justice and mercy. I would hope that we as Christians would try to make every facet of our lives incarnational.

Those who live incarnationally in any context should be able to apply the principles in this book, with discretion and creativity. However, the central focus and most direct application of this book is community-based incarnational ministry in urban poor neighborhoods. By "community-based," I mean the ministry that each of us has as a neighbor and community member, whether in your original (or accidental) hometown, or in a city that you have intentionally moved into in order to become a neighbor to its residents. Professional ministers will add community and church programming to their role in the neighborhood, but all Christians have plenty of opportunities to minister to those who live around them in less formal ways.

Where we live matters, and staying or putting ourselves in under-resourced communities can provide amazing opportunities to minister with a population whom God uniquely cherishes. This is the motivation behind an ancient and reviving movement to follow Christ not just wherever we happen to be, but specifically into the most underserved communities of the world.[8]

The Example of Christ

While Jesus came with a heart and message for the whole world, he leaned meaningfully toward those who were looked down upon by society—if society saw them at all. Christ's friends, like today's nearly *one billion* slum residents,[9] were looked down upon, considered unclean, and forgotten. Their communities were severely under-resourced and affected by bad politics, and they were often pressured to make choices that were considered immoral because of it.

Regardless of society's view of the poor of his day, Jesus prized them as they were: fully human and beloved by their Father. Jesus first showed this by coming into the world within the lower class, even though many expected the Messiah to be a powerful political leader.[10] Nor did Jesus aspire to leave urban poverty behind by becoming wealthy. In fact, preaching and manifesting the Kingdom of God among the poor remained a central part of his ministry.

Incarnational ministry follows the model of Jesus by choosing downward mobility. Hayes writes, "Taking Christ's example seriously has been the first step for generations of disciples to recover the fresh power of the Early Church."[11] Jesus lived among the people of his day, so contemporary ministers should also live among the people where they minister.

However, it is misguided at best to equate Jesus' incarnation with our own decision to leave wealthy communities for poorer ones. First, wealthy communities can hardly be compared to heaven. Second, Jesus is the only savior of the urban poor, and it is dangerous for human leaders to think they are fulfilling this exclusive role. We take after Jesus not as equals to Christ, but as followers of Christ and equals to our poor neighbors.

Urban Poverty Today

As large cities have become the main economic centers around the world, they have exploded in size. Countless people have migrated toward cities either because they are seeking economic opportunity, because their former rural homes are no longer livable, or both. As these cities are at full capacity, communities of all economic levels have sprawled out from city centers.

There are many terms to describe the poorest and most under-resourced of these communities: slum, ghetto, inner city, the hood, squatter, and settler are the common English terms. *Squatter* and *(informal) settler* refer to unofficial or unsanctioned communities, while the others can refer to official communities in a state of disrepair as well. Generally, these terms imply a high crime rate, though this labeling often has more to do with stereotypes than statistics. With these variables in mind, I will usually use *urban poor* because it is the most neutral and all-encompassing term.

In urban poor communities, public resources are stretched thin due to both booming populations and oppressive policies. Police, firefighters, and medical coverage are difficult to find and often lack quality. The poorer the residents, the less likely they are to make campaign contributions or devote scarce time and energy to self-advocacy, so they become less of a priority to receive standard government services. If residents did not purchase land or homes through official avenues, or if they built improvised homes without proper permits or without adhering to building codes, governments likely will not recognize their communities as legitimate. Their homes are often at risk of being destroyed by the government, as they were in Balic-Balic.

A healthy way of understanding urban poverty is to see it as a distortion of God's original design. It is one of the negative effects of the fall of humanity as described in the book of Genesis. This is not meant to disparage the poor themselves. Yes, the urban poor have their fair share of sins. But the existence of urban poor communities is an indictment on all of society.

Urban poor communities are not beyond redemption. The solution to urban poverty is not to demolish the neighborhoods and move the residents to middle-class housing. Much of ministry is discerning where God is already at work in a neighborhood and joining him in the journey. Christ has been at work in each community from its beginning. There are many positive aspects within urban poor communities, and they can be transformed into places of hope and faith in God.

Sharing space and struggles with our urban poor neighbors allows us to enter at least partially into the extraordinary communal bonds created through those challenges. Jude Tiersma, an incarnational leader in Los Angeles, writes, "The idea of incarnation, of walking with and dwelling among the people, of identifying with their sufferings, is essential for mission in the city."[12] The instant closeness that came with moving into Balic-Balic was especially noticeable in contrast to what I had experienced in my other, middle-class life. When I first moved in, the youth I had been working with didn't want me to live alone for safety reasons, so they each offered to stay with me a few days per week. I saw this as a great opportunity to become part of the fabric of the community. We studied the Bible and prayed, but mostly we just hung out together. One young man named Aileen ended up practically moving in with me, and he became one of my first professors of urban poverty. Content to eat a meal of rice and cooking oil, Aileen showed me true hunger for the first time in my life. None of us really knew how to cook and I didn't have much of a budget, so our meals together ended up consisting mostly of instant noodles with egg and rice, which we would eat together on the floor. For a mattress, we would unfold a cardboard box and put it on the floor. Then we'd all squish together and sleep. Having always slept in my own bed, it was quite an adjustment to wake up with someone's foot on my chest.

The young men's radical welcome of my own presence shows how community connection and identity can happen even in diverse neighborhoods with multiple ethnicities and even languages. A bond can form through the experience of sharing the same common spaces, receiving similar governmental services, and facing similar challenges. Of course, we can only hope to come closer to this community, praying for their grace and God's as we respectfully recognize that we cannot fully identify with the poverty experience by choosing into it.

POVERTY AND CHOICE. What makes voluntary poverty interesting and maybe problematic is that only those who are wealthy can choose into poverty. The very act of choosing to live in a poor community distinguishes you from the poor, as one of the symptoms of poverty is in fact the lack of choices. The poor cannot simply will themselves into resources the way we can will ourselves out of (and back into) them. College is unaffordable and difficult to prepare for in an under-resourced high school, so earning a degree is not usually a realistic option. Teenagers might even feel the need to work instead of finishing high school so they have money to buy food for themselves and their families. In particularly tough situations, teens and adults might choose crime as a way to provide for themselves.

When a person turns to crime, it reveals a much deeper issue than the sin of the criminal. As I walked the tracks to get home one evening, I was told that my good friend Aileen had been arrested for running drugs. I thought it was a joke that I didn't understand, but when I got home I found out that the rumor was true. We quickly went to the jail outside of Manila, where we found Aileen and his friends hungry and covered with painful rashes in a crowded, unsanitary cell. The look on his face confirmed what I already knew: Aileen was not a hardcore thug who enjoyed hurting people. He was simply trying to survive.

Picking up drugs for local dealers is one of the few jobs that is always available, and Aileen was caught in a situation where there were no other options in sight. You begin to sense the full extent of systemic injustice after watching someone sin in order to eat. After Aileen was released, we continued to live, study the Bible, pray, and worship together, asking God to reveal and provide more options for his life.

Lack of choice also contributes to the unhealthy habits that so often shape and shorten the lives of the urban poor. Smoking numbs hunger pains and is cheaper than buying food. Processed food is also cheap and readily available, while fresh fruits and vegetables are harder to find and more expensive. For example, Botocan residents can buy 20 tiny bags of chips for 20 pesos— about 50 cents! For that same amount, you could buy a small piece of fruit, if a vendor happens to come by. There is an unkind stereotype that the poor are ignorant or thoughtless about their own lives and the lives of their children. This simply isn't true. The pressure upon their lives is so immense that they are often operating in survival mode. All things considered, they are truly surviving quite impressively. We can love our poor neighbors by humbly offering emotional and practical support to make better but more difficult choices, and by occasionally joining them in efforts to make more choices available.

Facing Urban Stress: A Biblical Example

Life in any urban environment can be stressful, especially for those of us who grew up in more rural or suburban environments. Homes and people are densely packed, pollution abounds, traffic is terrible, sins and non-life-giving habits wait at every turn, violence shakes our sense of safety, nature is difficult to access, and last but not least, it is often *loud*. There are many wonderful things about city life too, but these factors will take their toll.

The Bible affirms that urban living can be essentially stressful. King David of Israel expressed his anxiety for life in Jerusalem in Psalm 55. This psalm speaks of the evils of life in the city:

> Give ear to my prayer, O God, and hide not yourself from my plea for mercy! Attend to me, and answer me; I am restless in my complaint and I moan, because of the noise of the enemy, because of the oppression of the wicked. For they drop trouble upon me, and in anger they bear a grudge against me. My heart is in anguish within me; the terrors of death have fallen upon me. Fear and trembling come upon me, and horror overwhelms me. And I say, "Oh, that I had wings like a dove! I would fly away and be at rest; yes, I would wander far away; I would lodge in the wilderness; I would hurry to find a shelter from the raging wind and tempest." Destroy, O Lord, divide their tongues; for I see violence and strife in the city. Day and night they go around it on its walls, and iniquity and trouble are within it; ruin is in its midst; oppression and fraud do not depart from its marketplace.[13]

David had a realistic view of the city. He lists some of the evils of Jerusalem, including violence, strife, iniquity, trouble, ruin, oppression, and fraud. We cannot have a utopian view of our city or any urban poor community, as evil does exist there. Like David, we need to be honest about what we see around us and what we face within the community.

The issues and problems in the city of Jerusalem overwhelmed David. He speaks of being totally overcome with fear. Fear is an appropriate and God-given response to a threat. We should not be ashamed of being afraid of real threats in our community. Fear, however, must not dominate us.

To solve the problem of fear and stress, David is tempted to run away. He wants to quit. When we are overwhelmed with the stresses from urban poor ministry, this is an attractive option. While we can physically quit and move away, more often the tendency is to quit emotionally, to withdraw and pull away. We can even reach the point where we no longer want to care. When we experience this burnout, we can follow David in being honest about our emotions.

David's Jerusalem sounds a lot like the community of Botocan and the city of Manila. There is an overall anxiety that is built into my daily life here. For instance, I recently got on the wrong jeepney (a type of public transportation) and had to find my way home from an unfamiliar part of the city after dark. Although I did not panic and my life was realistically not in a huge amount of danger, getting lost immersed me in my own sense of insecurity, overwhelm, and out-of-placeness within the context of the urban chaos of Botocan.

Anxiety grows in the face of troubling stories and statistics. Even in Botocan, which is usually safe, there have been murders in broad daylight. The city of Manila will occasionally experience moments of terror. When Zach was three years old, there was a bus bombing in the city, which became the major topic of conversation in Botocan. A few days later, Zach told me he wanted to tell me a story. He began, "Once upon a time there was a bus bombing." Everyone wants to think that their home is their sanctuary, but the urban poor (and those who live alongside them) do not have this privilege.

In our experience, the sources of urban stress can often change over time. In a prayer letter that I wrote after returning to Manila from two years in the United States, I wrote,

> Our first month here has been full of adjustments. So far the hardest have been spending so much time sitting in traffic, the heat, and the pollution. When I wipe the sweat off of my face, the tissue is black from the pollution. We are also adjusting to the relational culture of the Philippines. Meetings in the Philippines have no exact time. We spend the time sharing about our families and other casual talk before getting down to business. Even Ema, who grew up in the Philippines, is having reverse culture shock about how long our meetings are taking.

Years later, none of these are major causes of stress anymore. Traffic, heat, and pollution are still annoyances, but they are manageable, and we are learning to cope. The relational aspect of the culture is now something I enjoy. Long meetings are never fun, but being content just to enjoy people without being burdened by efficiency is one of the strengths of the urban poor. Today, our points of stress are totally different, and they should be, since we have moved to a new community and are now parents.

Sometimes it's hard to know how to respond to the evils we see. David's response was to call on God: "Cast your burden on the Lord, and he will sustain you; he will never permit the righteous to be moved."[14] This is a healthy response to the chaos and evil in our communities. Through prayer, God will sustain us. His strength will enable us to live righteously, even while surrounded by stress and violence.

Conclusion

Incarnational living has deep roots in Christian Scripture and tradition. Becoming a neighbor to the poor is a response to Christ's preference for the company of the outcasts of his day, who faced similar challenges and prejudices. Our urban poor neighbors around the globe face unique difficulties which are unimaginable to many in the middle class, and we follow Christ in coming alongside them in those difficulties. Moving into an urban poor environment can be stressful, especially as we come to terms with the suffering of the poor who live with little to no choice. However, it is often the best way to come alongside the poor and together engage the community for transformation.

[6] Jer. 29:5, ESV *(All Scriptural citations are from the English Standard Version.)*
[7] Jer. 29:7
[8] This push is sometimes called The New Friars Movement, after the Catholic and Episcopal role of an in-community monastic minister.
[9] Both the UN and the World Health Organization report more than eight hundred million people living in slum conditions in 2014.
[10] Jesus was born into poverty among animals (Luke 2:1-7). But the magi from the east, for example, assumed that the King of the Jews would be in the palace in Jerusalem among the elite (Matt. 2:1-12).
[11] John B. Hayes, *Sub-Merge: Living Deep in a Shallow World* (Ventura, CA: Regal Books, 2006), 115.
[12] Jude Tiersma, "What Does It Mean to Be Incarnational When We Are Not the Messiah?" in *God So Loves the City: Seeking a Theology for Urban Mission*, ed. Charles Van Engen and Jude Tiersma (Monrovia, CA: MARC, 1994), 18.
[13] Ps. 55:1-11
[14] Ps. 55:22

2

ASPECTS OF MEANINGFUL PRESENCE

MOVING INTO AN URBAN POOR COMMUNITY is not about being a savior to the poor. It is about living meaningfully in the new home that God has called you into. What does it look like to be physically present in an active, meaningful way? I will start with a few stories to illustrate how this plays out in my family's ministry. Then, we will focus in on some important elements that all of these stories share.

There are no office hours when you live in an urban poor community. Recently, we have been woken up late at night by children whose parents work night shifts. They get tired, and tired of waiting, and are often too hungry to fall asleep before their parents come home with food. I am glad that they know they're welcome to knock on our door when this happens. I have learned to keep canned tuna in the house so that we don't have to send them away—or start cooking at 11 p.m.!

Being present also means listening. God has given me the patience to sit and listen as people share their burdens with me, even as an introvert. People have "stopped by" to talk about their problems for two hours straight. Recently, a mother came by to tell Ema and me about her adolescent son, who had run away from home. She began crying as she told her story and shared the pain of not knowing where her son was. In that case, there was nothing we could do to help. But she thanked us for being the only ones with whom she felt comfortable sharing.

Sometimes being present allows us to come alongside our neighbors to solve problems together. In the midst of a major typhoon that flooded the streets and caused extensive power outages, our neighbor's six-year-old son swallowed a coin. The boy's mom was very distressed because other neighbors told her that it might be stuck in his heart. While this fear was medically untrue, there was a possibility that the coin would get stuck in his stomach or intestines. If that happened, he would need surgery.

The woman's husband was stranded at work, so Ema went with her to the emergency room. Eventually they found their way around flooded roads and arrived at the hospital, but with the power out the doctor could not take an x-ray. They returned home defeated, and Ema prayed that the coin would just go through his system like any food we eat. Sure enough, the next evening when he went to the bathroom, his mom found the coin. Many of the families around us recognized God working through Ema's prayer, and Ema's availability and emotional support helped to deepen our relationship with that family. As trust grew, the children became active in Sunday school and other aspects of church life.

Meaningful presence means acting in thoughtful love wherever God has brought you to engage your community for transformation. The following elements of meaningful presence may help you to ask questions about your own presence in your community.

Location

Place matters. Laying down roots in the city where God has us is the key to joining in with its transformation. Only those who are present, only those who are establishing their lives within the fabric of the community, can harness the unique power of the resident. Urban community developer Robert Lupton says that "those who occupy the land at this community crossroads, and the type of leadership they exert, will determine its quality of life."[15] Committed followers of Jesus, both local and relocated, can have a leavening effect on their home community, slowly turning the tide toward its transformation.

The residents of Botocan have much to teach us about treasuring our particular location. On more than one occasion, I have heard residents say they are "home sweet home in the USA: United Squatter Area." All residents, from young children to seniors, know they are squatters and do not officially own the land. They know that their homes could be demolished, just like Balic-Balic. And yet, as long as they have the choice to stay, they will. Even when the government offers them the opportunity to buy legal housing in a distant relocation site, most do not want to move. Botocan is more than a place to live as a last resort. It is home. It is where their friends and family gather, where their history has developed, and where their sense of belonging is centered.

Even with the standing threat of demolition, the community members have invested in their homes and businesses. With little governmental assistance, residents will use their own limited resources to fix problems associated with common space. The walkway near our home and church had an area that flooded every time it rained, so the owner of our rented home concreted it. There is also a sense of concern for the common good of the community. Residents keep the walkways in front of their homes clean and spend money on potted plants to provide some greenery in the midst of wood, scrap metal, and concrete.

Botocan is also very important to residents in that it provides the setting for numerous neighborhood events, such as birthday parties, community meetings, and colorful Christmas celebrations. The summer basketball league consists of all local players who meet at the court at the center of town. They develop their own teams and get special permission from the government to go door to door throughout Botocan collecting money for uniforms and supplies. Thus the league is truly a community effort, and a central part of Botocan's identity as a place.

Many urban poor residents will live, shop, work, and go to school locally. Likewise, it is natural for them to also go to church and join a Bible study locally. The residents of Botocan are living in their urban slum, with all its problems and pains, in a purposeful way. They have created memories that emotionally connect them to their community, and no other place is quite like it. These are the elements of place that are not visible to outside visitors.

Moving in allows the minister to see and experience everything about a place, but it also allows the community to see the minister's life with clarity. By sharing a location with the urban poor, the lives of incarnational leaders are displayed for the community to observe. Ema and I have experienced that our neighbors watch us not only at our best, but also at our worst. We become real people, rather than untouchable priests, angels, or saints. And that is where our witness is. We are able to serve as living examples of followers of Jesus, who try to respond to our shared struggles as Christ would have us respond. Being present by moving into the community and becoming part of its fabric is an essential part of this incarnational witness.

One way to be more meaningfully present is to learn about the neighborhood, starting with knowledge from the residents themselves. I have talked with a wide variety of Botocan residents about their experiences, from seniors who were some of the original inhabitants, to young teens who are just beginning to shape their community's culture. I have also done research at local government offices in order to know the community's demographics better, and I read books on its history. When I first lived in Manila, I would travel around on public transportation and write down the names of the streets that I passed. This allowed me to find out where I had been on a map and get to know the physical layout of the city. All of this has helped me to know and to love both my community and city.

Being meaningfully present in your location also implies a sense of permanence. Permanence is the mindset that says, "I am here—as a resident, not a visitor." One doesn't need to make a lifetime commitment to make a home somewhere, but an incarnational leader must lay down more roots than a Christian tourist.

An important way to create a sense of permanence is to invest money, time, and energy into your place the neighborhood. Some incarnational leaders choose to buy homes in their urban poor communities. Some have bought squatter property, while others have purchased property with legal land titles. Either way, they are saying to both themselves and their neighbors that they intend to be in the community for a significant amount of time.

In many urban poor communities, the option to purchase a home or property is just not available. Either the whole community is made up of rental units or there are legal restrictions on who can purchase property. In some nations such as the Philippines, only citizens are allowed to buy property. But renters can cultivate a sense of permanence in other ways. We have literally planted a rooftop garden on the third floor of our place. We have also invested in pigs that are raised by a family in Botocan. Pigs take several months to mature, so buying them signals commitment to stay for at least that long. These very physical anchors are coupled with our many roles in the church and in the community so that both we and our neighbors are constantly reminded that we identify deeply as long-term residents of Botocan.

Engagement

Though location is important, even proudly and sincerely sharing a zip code with the urban poor is not in itself incarnational. Some wealthy or middle-class people are drawn to urban poor locations because they perceive their cultures to be hardcore, anti-establishment, and/or especially authentic. The cheaper housing costs may also attract some to rent in an urban poor community so they can spend their income in other ways, or save up for the future. Similarly, relocating to an urban poor community for the purpose of studying urban poverty, the local culture, or a foreign language often leads to little more than anthropological exercise. None of these motivations for being present are necessarily bad, but they are not incarnational ministry.

It is possible, and maybe too common, to live in an urban poor community hiding behind locked doors, not knowing one's neighbors, and not engaging the community for transformation. It is also just as possible to live in one urban poor community and be so involved in school, work, or even ministry in another region that the neighborhood in which one lives is little more than a place to sleep. Again, this is not a negative, except that it is a huge missed opportunity. Those living among the urban poor must humbly recognize that our presence alone is not a ministry—that living next door is not the same as being a neighbor.

Engagement means becoming a neighbor, becoming involved in the civic life of a community. It will include intentional activity both as a community member, and as a vocational minister or lay church leader. We will delve more deeply into those two roles in chapters five and six. For now, let me cite some examples from Botocan to spark your imagination for creative community engagement.

The residents of Botocan are some of the kindest and most helpful neighbors we have ever had. The Bible studies that we host always end with everyone sharing their prayer requests. One night, a high school student asked for prayer that he would wake up in time for school. Two others not only volunteered to pray for him, but also offered to help him wake up! One would keep him accountable by making sure that he was not hanging out in town past 9:00 p.m. Another man, who wakes up at 4:00 a.m. for work, offered to stop by and wake him up each morning. The citizens of Botocan are constantly going out of their way to help each other excel.

Another way the residents of Botocan are engaged in the transformation of their community is by sharing resources in times of need. When one resident is hospitalized and unable to pay the hospital bills, others will chip in to help pay so that the family is not crushed by debt. This has occurred numerous times during our stay in Botocan and shows the interconnectedness of the residents. When this happens, we will chip in an amount similar to what other residents are giving. This is both because we genuinely don't have a lot of resources ourselves, and because we want the giving to remain the communal activity that it should be.

Engagement can also mean developing systems that work for the community. The residents of Botocan have put together a very efficient fire protection system. By sending runners with megaphones, information can be sent throughout the community within a matter of minutes. During one false alarm, the hose was connected to the local fire hydrant and the water was turned on before they realized there was no fire. When one considers all of the winding walkways in Botocan, this is an incredible feat. Residents are engaging the community to help make Botocan a safer and better place to live. Joining or helping to initiate community self-protection systems like this is a great way to be involved in the community.

Some of my friends back home are surprised to hear that both the citizens and the local government of Botocan have a deep sense of civic engagement. Election days are important community events, and long lines of chatting neighbors spill out from the voting booths as they wait. All of the elected officials live in Botocan, so they also have a stake in the community. The local government in Botocan has even partnered with our church to sponsor Alternative Learning System, the Philippine equivalent of a GED in the United States. We are able to host these classes on Saturdays to prepare dropout youth, along with a few older adults, for the high school equivalency exam.

Engagement isn't about building community from scratch or recreating it in your image while you remain unchanged. It's about joining, learning from, and offering what you can to the thriving systems that are already in place. David, an incarnational leader with Servants to Asia's Urban Poor (SERVANTS), describes this process as being in sync with the rhythms of the community.[16] Incarnational leaders need to learn how to be in the community, connected to its life, even as we recognize and respect that we will never be able to engage as indigenous citizens.

Love at the Center

The one element that most clearly defines incarnational ministry is a genuine, active love of our neighbors and the community we live in. Our engagement in the community needs to be rooted in love for God, others, and ourselves. Paul taught the Christians in Corinth the centrality of love in good works: "If I give away all I have, and if I deliver up my body to be burned, but have not love, I gain nothing."[17] We can do all kinds of services and programs with our neighbors, but as Paul reminds us, without love our works mean nothing. It is only through love that our engagement can be genuine.

The alternative to being rooted in love is hypocritical or performance ministry. We cannot visit the community, put on a righteous front, share about God, and then go home and have a violent fight with our family. This is never an acceptable thing to do, but in the close proximity of the urban poor community, the minister simply cannot get away with it. Whenever Ema and I have an argument, it does not even matter that we maintain calm speaking voices. All of our neighbors hear us through the thin walls, and our love and respect for each other must show through even as we disagree. Likewise, if our ministry routine was becoming a cover for bitter and unloving feelings toward the community, it would only be a matter of time before everyone around us began to see the signs.

Of course, short fuses will happen. It is easy to feel love for an impoverished child in a photograph, but when that same child turns out to be the most out-of-control, bratty kid you've ever met, she is no longer so easy to love. Some of the children in our neighborhood smell like they have not taken a bath in a month, and their hair is crawling with lice. It takes extra love and compassion to play with them—a love and compassion I do not always have.

Thankfully, we get opportunities each day to love again. On one occasion, a child followed me outside Botocan, so I scolded him and sent him home. I should have sent him home in a significantly nicer manner than I did. Fortunately, he was not easily offended, and I have been able to love him better at other times.

And what a testament to Christ when his love shows through over time! It is through a growing relationship with Jesus that we are able to make the emotional commitment needed to invest in relationships with our family members, teammates, and neighbors, who inevitably bring all of their brokenness and messiness into these relationships. Centering our ministry in loving Christ through our neighbor and our neighbor through Christ prevents us from becoming task oriented and burning out.

BEYOND SIMPLE LIVING. When material possessions are at the center of our life, love usually isn't. The Bible teaches over and over again that possessions aren't meant to be greedily held, but put in the service of community relationships. Some examples include the Old Testament command that reapers were to leave the edges of the fields and what was missed during the harvest for the poor.[18] John the Baptist taught the crowds about sharing our possessions through economic repentance: "Whoever has two tunics is to share with him who has none, and whoever has food is to do likewise."[19] We must follow this command by leaving behind the race to own the biggest and the best, and by loosely holding onto the things that we do have.

The urban poor can show us how wasteful we are with things we normally do not even think about. Small things like eating hot leftovers and drinking cold water are luxuries that many urban poor live without. The urban poor can teach incarnational leaders that living without certain material possessions can actually be liberating. When material distractions are removed, it is amazing how wide the door is opened for spiritual growth—and for seeing what really matters in life. We may even discover that we have legitimate needs that we should not feel guilty about.

Likewise, joining our neighbors in a life of simplicity helps to undermine the pressure on the poor to measure their success by how many things they have (or haven't) accumulated. Sadly, it is not only the affluent who face an overwhelming bombardment of materialism and commercialism. The urban poor can be just as materialistic as anyone else. I once spoke with a woman in her early twenties as she was fetching water. Her home was about the size of a twin bed. Her possessions included a small sleeping mat, a small box of clothes, a few books and school supplies, a radio, a cell phone, and a 25-gallon water drum. After noticing the water drum was in the far end of her room, I asked about the difficulty of carrying buckets of water over her sleeping mat to fill it. She told me that she did not keep water in the drum; it was for her purses. This young woman was struggling to finish her schooling and did not have enough money to eat, but it seemed as though owning more purses than she could properly store helped her to feel less poor, perhaps less ashamed of her poverty. By choosing to live without excess things voluntarily, we can give a persuasive argument that poverty is not shameful and that owning as much as possible is not the most satisfying goal in life.

By limiting the number of time-consuming possessions, such as television sets and computer games, incarnational leaders are able to spend their evenings in community with neighbors. Having less encourages the mutual sharing of possessions between the minister and his or her neighbors and lets them relate more equally. It is extremely difficult to avoid creating a patron/client relationship when living a middle-class lifestyle among the urban poor, but living a relatively similar lifestyle allows peer friendships to develop. One incarnational leader used to wash his clothes at a neighbor's home since that neighbor owned a washing machine. Eventually, he was given a washing machine as a gift. While he does appreciate being able to wash clothes whenever he wants to, it resulted in losing relational time with his neighbor.[20]

Despite its importance, rejecting the material does not mean one's life is instead centered in love. In fact, material simplicity can easily become a source of self-righteousness and burnout stress if it drifts toward asceticism. It can also lead to missed opportunities. Hospitality, a key element of living meaningfully in a community, is challenging when the incarnational leader's home is so bare the only place to sit is on the floor, or if there are not enough plates and silverware to host meals.

Rejecting legitimate material needs can also limit or cut short a family's ability to minister. I know one family whose child was allergic to her own sweat. If the family had insisted on strict material simplicity as the only option for their home, they might have endangered their child, been forced to send her to live with relatives, or quickly moved back to the sub-urbs. Instead, they installed an air conditioning unit in their otherwise urban poor home. Though it was expensive, it made their continued ministry possible, and it allowed them to invite neighbors to come enjoy some relief from hot days as well. Leaders do not need to feel guilty over possessions that are legitimate personal or ministerial needs. Love for God and our neighbors, rather than rejection of possessions, must be at the center of our ministry.

BEYOND IDENTIFICATION. Part of how we express our love for the world's poor is by being willing to enter into many aspects of their suffering with them. Identification—the mindset of becoming one with the poor, being able to relate to their poverty, and struggling with them in solidarity—does have validity. Leaders usually choose to live like the poor around them in an attempt to make the statement, "I want to be one of you. I am on your side." The goal of identification is to break down the human-related barriers to the gospel, to fully know the poverty and suffering of the urban poor, and to learn from the many positive aspects of urban poor cultures.

Identification is closely connected with the process of contextualization, or customizing teaching and programming to fit the experiences of the community. Living among the poor helps incarnational leaders to understand the culture of the urban poor and thus it helps in the communication of the gospel. It was through observation of my urban poor neighbors' communication patterns that I was able to integrate those same communication patterns both in facilitating Bible studies, and in social conversations. Our lives and ministries must come closer to the experiences of our poor neighbors if we expect connection or mutual growth.

Despite these benefits, identification is a dangerous end goal for an incarnational leader. It often amounts to attempting to imitate the experience of the poor. Tim Chester argues against incarnational ministry because he equates it with identification. Chester writes, "Incarnational mission equates culture with 'artefacts' [sic]. The focus becomes on what you wear or do."[21] Associating incarnational leadership with matching external behaviors or appearances is materialistic in its own way. For incarnational leaders among the urban poor, the stress on identification is not so much on external lifestyle similarity as it is on learning to consider and deeply empathize with the perspectives and experiences of their poor neighbors.

Even so, this attitude does not recognize that having the same amount of possessions or income as the poor is only a small portion of the poverty experience. Liberation theologian and incarnational leader Gustavo Gutierrez writes that incarnational leaders from the middle and upper classes will "never reach the point of real identification with the life of the poor."[22] We cannot truly simulate the experience of poverty, as it has many dimensions that I cannot and should not necessarily enter into. I do not have the stress of not knowing whether I will be evicted for unpaid rent, nor do I live with a violent relative who is both physically and verbally abusive. I do not know the limitation and embarrassment of being non-literate, or of not finishing high school. Unlike most of my poor neighbors whose social relationships are limited to people of similar social class, I have friends who are wealthy and could help me out if a major need arose. Finally, even if I never exercise it, I have the option to flash my passport and leave if life becomes too hard or if the country becomes unsafe. It would be insulting to my neighbors to pretend that we are in the exact same situation.

Releasing identification as an end goal also allows us to accommodate for our own legitimate needs and values without unnecessary anxiety. For example, an old ankle injury has limited my ability to join the basketball games that are so central to the community. Instead of forcing myself to play (and possibly landing myself in crutches), I support from the sidelines when I can. If a popular dish makes you sick for a week every time you eat it, perhaps you shouldn't eat it. And while imitating the many positive aspects of the local culture can bring a lot of joy and personal growth, every culture in every part of the world also has aspects that should not be imitated. An incarnational leader is not someone who watches hours of daytime television with his neighbors or makes herself sick on alcohol and drugs at local parties in order to fully join the community. The inability or decision not to imitate the urban poor in some respects does not mean one is less incarnational as a minister. In fact, sometimes love is more boldly and radically communicated by finding ways to maintain relationships across differences.

Rather than focus on fully identifying with the urban poor, Michael Duncan of SERVANTS says we should focus on "participating with the poor."[23] We can appreciate the ways in which we are insiders and peers, rather than dwelling on the ways we may always be outsiders. For example, we often get invited to children's birthday parties because of our young sons, Zach and Ezra. As we talk with the other moms and dads, we don't feel like we're "infiltrating" the parent group as part of our ministry—we simply *are* parents! Our relationships to the community are not staged; they are genuine friendships based in spontaneous shared meals and common concerns. We honestly acknowledge differences in background and privilege, but our lifestyle does help to lower barriers that would prevent us from relating to our neighbors in reciprocally loving and caring relationships.

Conclusion

Meaningful presence in an urban poor community means making yourself at home there. It means taking interest in and becoming familiar with the complex identity of a neighborhood. It means building relationships with neighbors and becoming part of the social fabric of the community. Finally, it means keeping love firmly at the center of all of your activities, relationships, and decisions. These elements, rather than the external elements of looking or living like your poor neighbors, are truly at the center of the incarnational leader's presence and purpose in the community.

[15] Robert D. Lupton, *Renewing the City: Reflections on Community Development and Urban Renewal* (Downers Grove, IL: InterVarsity Press, 2005), 222. Though I agree with Lupton's ideas about meaningful presence, residents in urban poor communities are often the victims of political occupation; therefore I avoid his term *a theology of occupation*.

[16] Interview with David Cross, October 18, 2011. Tanay, Philippines.

[17] 1 Cor. 13:3

[18] Lev. 19:9-10, 23:22, and Deut. 24:19-22

[19] Luke 3:10-11

[20] Interview with Kevin Blue, August 6, 2011. Los Angeles.

[21] Tim Chester, "Why I Don't Believe in Incarnational Mission," *Tim Chester Blog*, July 19, 2008, accessed December 11, 2015, *bit.ly/timchesterincarnational*.

[22] Gustavo Gutierrez, *We Drink from Our Own Wells: The Spiritual Journey of a People*, trans. Matthew J. O'Connell (London: SCM Press, 1987), 126.

[23] Michael Duncan, *The Incarnational Approach* (Christchurch: SERVANTS, 1991), 6.

3

DESIRED OUTCOMES

THERE IS A DEEP, ESSENTIAL VALUE in simply being present in an urban poor community, and we can expect to have many wonderful and meaningful moments as we do so. However, it is also helpful to keep in mind some general end goals that we are working toward. This is not a personal or political agenda, but it is how we expect God will move if he is meaningfully involved in our ministries.

A woman in our community once told a friend that she saw religion as very destructive. When our newly planted church was mentioned in response, she remarked, "I take my hat off to Aaron's church because they are not disruptive. On second thought, they are disruptive, but in a good way—like osmosis."

Incarnational ministry is very much like osmosis. Osmosis is when two cells touch each other and the molecules of one cell pass through the cell membranes into the other cell. In the same way, incarnational leaders expect to see change for the better in both themselves and the community. This does not mean that things happen without effort or intention. However, it is through coming close with others in their celebrations and struggles that we are able to influence each other's lives for the better.

Kingdom Transformation

While the word *transformation* can sometimes be applied to individual, internal experiences, that is not what I mean when I use it. Transformation is when a society, city, or neighborhood moves closer to the vision of the Kingdom of God, or in the words of God as recorded by Isaiah, a new heaven and new earth:

> For behold, I create new heavens and a new earth, and the former things shall not be remembered or come into mind. But be glad and rejoice forever in that which I create; for behold, I create Jerusalem to be a joy, and her people to be a gladness. I will rejoice in Jerusalem and be glad in my people; no more shall be heard in it the sound of weeping and the cry of distress. No more shall there be in it an infant who lives but a few days, or an old man who does not fill out his days, for the young man shall die a hundred years old, and the sinner a hundred years old shall be accursed. They shall build houses and inhabit them; they shall plant vineyards and eat their fruit. They shall not build and another inhabit; they shall not plant and another eat; for like the days of a tree shall the days of my people be, and my chosen shall long enjoy the work of their hands. They shall not labor in vain or bear children for calamity, for they shall be the offspring of the blessed of the Lord, and their descendants with them. Before they call I will answer; while they are yet speaking I will hear. The wolf and the lamb shall graze together; the lion shall eat straw like the ox, and dust shall be the serpent's food. They shall not hurt or destroy in all my holy mountain.[24]

This is a picture of the fullness of the Kingdom of God. It provides a vision Jesus' followers should be praying for and working toward. In this vision, there will be no cries of distress. The city will be safe to walk day or night. Women will not have to fear sexual predators in the alleyways. Infants will not die. Pregnant women will receive proper prenatal care, and babies will receive pediatric care. There will be safe drinking water and decent sanitation. Food will be safe. People will be able to maintain physical fitness and health care will be available. There will be just economic policies. People will be able to live off the fruit of their labor. There will be peace. Wars will cease. Domestic violence will no longer terrorize families. Neighbors will no longer fight. People will live out their days.

It is dangerously false to think that incarnational leaders are supposed to arrive on the scene and begin carrying out this grand vision. Both local and relocated leaders take a small part in a vision that is ultimately God's. The educational background, connections, and political privilege of middle-class westerners must meet the experience, insight, and vital creativity of civic, religious, and community leaders already in the neighborhood. In other words, the assets of middle-class leaders should not be embraced for their own goals or self-satisfaction, but they can be meaningfully leveraged in support of a community's initiatives. Kingdom transformation is never the leader's show; his or her visibility is simply one more asset that he or she can put in service of the community.

One key aspect of transformation is pushing back against injustice. One afternoon, a group of police entered our neighborhood without a warrant and arrested two men for stabbing and robbing a woman the night before. One of those arrested was Jio, a member of our church. After talking to the police, another church leader and I discovered that they had no real evidence against Jio. The victim even said he did not look like her attacker. But the police still did not want to release him. Violent crimes need to be solved, and the police felt they had to make an arrest regardless of whether or not the person was actually guilty. After pressing into several discussions with different officers, we were informed that Jio would be released. In the neighborhood, word spread quickly. Knowing how intractably faulty the justice system can be here, many people were surprised to see him. One man told me, "You have a powerful God."

Community transformation can include positive changes in many areas, from affordable housing, to education, to new businesses. Ema has been sampling various income-generating projects for some of the women in the neighborhood, including helping one woman start a burger business. Generous friends helped by providing start-up capital to purchase most of the major supplies and an interest-free loan to cover the remaining expenses. The vision for the burger business is that it will provide a steady income for the owner, and she will be able to hire college students so they can earn while studying. None of this was Ema's idea; she is just supporting however she can. Transformation requires the creativity not just of the incarnational leader, but of the community as well.

New Followers of Christ

While we want to move away from a salvation-driven missionary model that is only concerned about how many people say the sinner's prayer, it is good and right to celebrate whenever someone begins or renews a relationship with God through Christ. The leader should expect to participate in God's movement toward the poor in this way. As John B. Hayes writes, "We validate hope by showing our neighbors that we entrust ourselves to the same upside-down gospel that we proclaim."[25] Our witness as Christian neighbor-ministers can contribute directly to residents' new relationships with Christ. Over time, the evidence of God in the lives of these new followers will in turn begin to speak to their neighbors and family members.

Before meeting Jesus, Jio was a hardened criminal. His legal aid called him a hopeless case and thought he would spend the rest of his life in prison. One evening, Jiovane knocked on our door. He introduced himself and said that he noticed how transformed some of the people who attended our church had been. He told me that he too wanted his life changed. Jiovane began attending church, small group, prayer meeting, and every other Bible study in our church. He left his gang and committed his life to Jesus. I later asked Jio what had attracted him to our church, and he shared this story with me.

> Before I became involved in Botocan Bible Christian Fellowship (BBCF), I was a thug. I worked as a thief, holding people up and robbing them. I was in and out of jail so many times. In jail, I joined a gang. That is the only way to survive in jail.
>
> I saw the difference that Jesus made in the lives of my friends who began attending BBCF. They used to be just like me. They would get drunk every night, and were always making trouble. They were thieves and trouble-makers. Now when I see them, they are different. They talk differently, and they have hope. I noticed that their lives were different. It is not like they are perfect. Sometimes they still get drunk, but now it is only once a month.
>
> I knew that my life needed to change. Being in and out of jail is no way to live. Last New Year's, I was drunk and setting off fireworks. One of them blew up in my hand. When I went to the hospital the doctor told me I would lose my hand. I praise God that I did not lose

my hand and although three fingers are disfigured, I can still use my hand. I thanked God for letting me keep it. That was the point when I knew that I needed to change.

When my gang friends would hire a prostitute, I began to think about my two daughters. I no longer wanted to be part of that because I saw the prostitute not as a sex object, but as someone's daughter. When I left my gang, they respected my decision and did not retaliate against me.

When I got involved in BBCF, my life began to change. I have been welcomed in the church. I know that it is not a sin to drink moderately, but I want to stop totally so that I can be a good testimony for BBCF. I know that my old gang friends are watching and observing my life. They have seen the positive change in my life and have realized that there is another way to live.[26]

Jiovane's actions have become a testimony to his old gang friends, who are seeing the difference Jesus has made in his life. I believe that the power of his story will continue to cause ripples throughout the community, causing more people to wonder what Jesus might have for their own lives.

Personal Growth

Ema and I expect to see some spiritual growth within ourselves and our sons as we minister as a family. All in all, the experience of living in an urban poor community has a decidedly positive impact on incarnational leaders' walk with God. Seventy-four percent of the leaders that I interviewed believe they have grown markedly closer to God during their time among the poor.[27] In the midst of the pain of urban poor life, incarnational leaders are able to become sensitive to the work of God in their lives.

When I first heard someone discussing the positive aspects of urban poor life on our walk with God, it actually discouraged me. I had struggled so much in my own relationship with God during my first years. It took several months of reflection to convince me that urban poor life did in fact have spiritual benefits. Since then, I have had times of feeling especially close to God in an urban poor community—times of corporate prayer, prayer walks through the neighborhood, or encouraging conversation. I have also come to realize that moving into a slum community is an act of worship. It is a physical reminder that I love Jesus more than comfort and security. It is one way to manifest the fact that Jesus is truly my treasure.

Living in an urban poor context provides countless opportunities to obey God's Word, and to see the fruit of that obedience. Scripture commands Jesus' followers to "rejoice with those who rejoice, weep with those who weep."[28] In many ways, all of incarnational ministry is in pursuit of obedience to this command. But sometimes, we get to obey it very directly.

One day, Amor showed up at our door in tears. She had just returned from yet another disappointing conversation with her mom. She had gone to ask her mother for money to pay the graduation fees required by her high school, but her mom instead began yelling at Amor and told her to drop out of school in order to work.

Amor expressed her desire to finish her last two months of high school and find a good job. As she explained all of this, Ema just sat and cried with her. We offered her our support and together came up with a plan to allow her to graduate. Amor would ask other relatives to help cover her financial needs until graduation. When all else failed, we would also help. Eventually we came up with a work-for-food agreement to ensure that Amor would not have to go to school hungry.

Ema and I planned to attend the graduation in support of Amor, as both of her parents said they would not be present. We were shocked when her mom showed up just hours before, suddenly overcome with pride that her daughter had become the very first person in her family to graduate from high school. We joyfully returned the tickets Amor had given us, happy to know that Amor would receive her diploma as her mother applauded her accomplishment. By obediently risking empathy with Amor's pain, we were also able to share in her moment of victory.

Growing in love and obedience of God should never be a source of pride, but it can be a source of joy. I believe that we are happiest and most fulfilled in active relationship to God. For those of us who are called to urban poor ministry, the spiritual cost of not following this call is too great, and the many spiritual rewards of following it are important aspects of sustaining a lifelong ministry.

Conclusion

Ministry within an urban poor community can be vibrant and exciting. An incarnational minister should not mistake the visible results of ministry with the true ministry of consistent meaningful presence. However, positive outcomes in the community, church, and the individual are to be expected when we are genuinely engaging. Recognizing these outcomes can be a key part of reflecting on and sustaining a long-term ministry.

[24] Isa. 65:17-25

[25] John B. Hayes, *Sub-Merge: Living Deep in a Shallow World* (Ventura, CA: Regal Books, 2006), 116.

[26] Interview with Jiovane Amplayohan, July 3, 2011. Quezon City, Philippines.

[27] See Appendix B for more results and discussion from my dissertation research.

[28] Rom. 12:15

4

COUNTING THE COSTS

WHILE URBAN POOR COMMUNITIES are fruitful, exciting, and often beautiful places to participate in God's coming Kingdom, there are very real costs to relocating there. Living in poverty is painful and difficult, and the reality of urban poor life can feel like a massive burden on the shoulders of an incarnational leader. Being realistic about this toll throughout the decision-making process is crucial to a sustainable ministry.

The following are some common costs that incarnational leaders face. While we generally need to be prepared to embrace all of them, the extent to which each comes into play will depend on the community and modes of ministry that you choose. Each leader will need to prayerfully determine whether any of these costs should be curbed or avoided when making choices that will shape ministry.

Time

As part of my discernment process before moving into an urban poor community, I estimated the decision would shorten my life by about ten years. Though there are some very elderly people in our community, the stress, risk of violence, and health factors such as pollution may all contribute to a decline in my own longevity. I went into this ministry fully aware of that risk.

We also have less control over how we spend the time that is ours when we are in an urban poor community. Since we do not own a car, we are totally dependent on public transportation. On the occasional days when there are transportation strikes, we either have to totally cancel our plans to leave the community, or wait an exceptionally long time for a strikebreaking jeepney to pass by. Even on normal days, we can spend a significant amount of time waiting for an empty jeepney. This means simple errands can take up a good portion of the day. The amount of "wasted" time felt like a huge cost as I transitioned from the relatively fast-paced and efficient routines of my other life.

In Botocan, reading and studying are not considered work, so it is difficult to explain to my neighbors that I need to be left alone in order to complete these tasks. Since relationships are so highly valued, spending hours every evening just hanging out with friends is expected. Loitering at the local basketball court is a common way to spend evenings. While relationships are built in this way, tangible results are slow in coming. This can be frustrating after a while because the ministry does not seem to be productive. Fruitful incarnational ministry is heavily relational, and therefore time-consuming.

Sleep

One obvious example of urban stress in my ministry is exhaustion. Noisy neighbors can determine what time you are able to fall asleep and what time you wake up. Functioning for a full day of family and ministry responsibilities on minimal sleep is stressful. The following is a recent excerpt from my journal.

> Yesterday morning, I was awakened at 5:30 a.m. by a neighbor who thought that everyone around him wanted to listen to the radio. I stayed in bed until I realized that I was not going to fall back to sleep. This happened to be the beginning of an extra busy day. After multiple hours of teaching and meetings, I went to bed, quite exhausted. However, there was a party at the nearby basketball court. The bass from the speaker felt like it was right outside our window. I could feel the vibrations from the bass. I tried earplugs to no avail. I was only able to sleep off and on until the party finally ended.
>
> Unfortunately, this sleep was short-lived. My neighbor, who had been drinking, was angry about something. He stood right outside of his door, which happens to be right outside of our bedroom window, and began to curse and yell as loud as he could. I woke up thinking, "What's happening?" In the distance, I could hear shouts from neighbors telling him they were trying to sleep. This only made him yell louder. I began to wonder who he was mad at, when all of a sudden it sounded like he was trying to kick down our door. Ema and I both sat up. Suddenly, his wife came out and began to hit him, asking him why he was waking up all the neighbors and telling him that he was the only person she knew that could get in a fight without an opponent.
>
> Things quieted down, but I was unable to sleep. I found out in the morning he had kicked his ladder

that went up to his roof. It came down and crashed into our door. While I am relieved that he did not intentionally try to kick in our door, I am exhausted because I did not get enough rest. By the way, today is my birthday.

Depending on your personal needs and stage in life, lack of sleep may be more or less of an issue. When I first began to minister, the vivacity of my neighborhood was an enjoyable part of urban poor life. Every night was like a street party. Everyone would hang out in the evenings, blasting loud music and talking until early morning. Now that I am in my later thirties with children, lack of sleep has become a major cost.

Neatness

Life among the poor is often messy, and we sometimes have to literally get our hands dirty. Those who find a lot of comfort in order and control might experience this cost as especially painful.

The small creek that intersected Balic-Balic was an open sewer with no plant life. Although it was barely a foot deep, the bottom could not be seen because of the black, smelly water. Simply getting splashed by a few drops of that water was an unpleasant experience. Yet, one afternoon I found myself drenched in it.

We were walking along the creek on the way back from a prayer meeting when an electric box exploded and started a fire. Residents began running and screaming. Ema quickly went to find the group of Americans who were with us for Servant Partners' new staff training. I hurried home to move our passports and computer files to a safe place. Once everyone

53

was accounted for, the Servant Partners team and I joined the bucket brigade to put out the fire. In the frantic rush, sewage water splashed everywhere as we passed buckets. The thought that the water might actually make the fire worse did cross my mind, but thankfully it was effective. By the time the fire was under control, I was totally drenched. My best Sunday clothes were now dripping with stench. My hair was soaked, and I was doing my best to keep the water out of my mouth. I looked around and saw that just about every able male in the community was likewise drenched.

I was not able to take a bath until later that evening. I soaped and rinsed twice and rubbed my arms and legs with rubbing alcohol, but I could still feel and smell the stuff in my skin.

Was it worth getting drenched in sewage water to help save squatter homes from being destroyed by fire? Of course it was! It was my own community (including my own house!) that I helped save. It was worth it because I was able to get dirty with my neighbors and build deeper bonds with them. However, there is no denying that this event was unpleasant, and it's representative of the chaos and stink that sometimes comes with living in a slum.

Material Security

Even a very sincere middle-class Christian might experience a certain ache at the idea of leaving behind, well, *their stuff*. As we have discussed throughout this book, incarnational ministry doesn't involve owning absolutely nothing. However, it does involve eliminating excess that separates us from the poor, and holding a loose enough grip on the things that we keep.

One pastor who commuted to his urban poor church confided in me that he did not live in the community because of his possessions. In his words, "How can I enjoy my giant flat screen television if I look out the window and see poverty all around me?" He recognizes that if he moved into a squatter community, he would have to make some lifestyle changes that he does not want to make. Regardless of what you think of this excuse, at least he was honest. This pastor touched on an important cost related to incarnational ministry among the urban poor.

Jesus had a lot to say about how we treat our possessions. The Parable of the Rich Fool in Luke 16 teaches us about not storing up treasures on earth, but rather in heaven through giving to the poor.[29] Followers of Jesus cannot become too attached to possessions because we know they are not ultimately ours—and because we never know when we will lose them.

THEFT. One of the costs that needs to be counted in urban poor ministry is being robbed. While only sixteen percent of surveyed incarnational leaders have been pick-pocketed, thirty-three percent have had their house broken into.[30] This has happened to us several times. One of the most disturbing times was when we were all home. Early one Monday morning, Zach was playing with two other neighborhood kids, and Ema and I were talking in the bedroom. Two young men in their early twenties walked by our house and stopped in front of the door. They must have thought no adults were home because one of the men walked in, put on my sandals, and walked out. I stepped into the doorway and asked him why he was wearing my sandals. He started to run, so I gave chase, running

55

barefoot and shouting, "Robber! Robber!" My sandals were several sizes too big for him, so he quickly threw them back. I stopped chasing him and explained to all the on-looking neighbors what had happened. I felt embarrassed for chasing him for only a pair of sandals and said that I should have just let him keep them. My neighbors rebuked me, telling me that I should have chased him until he was caught, because someone who enters homes with children in plain sight is a danger to the community.

Having possessions stolen comes with the territory. The only thing of value in our squatter home is a laptop computer. I constantly make backup files, not because I am afraid that the computer will crash, but because I do not want to lose the files if the computer is stolen. We also do not keep certain documents in our home. I keep all of our original birth certificates, marriage certificate, and other important documents with relatives. Between break-ins and fires, I do not want to have to spend days trying to replace important documents.

Ema and I have also been robbed by people on the street more times than we can remember. One day, Ema was on a jeepney when she felt a sharp pain in her side. The passenger seated next to her was pressing a knife against her ribs, demanding her bracelet. Ema took it off and gave it to him as all of the other passengers just watched. He then exited the jeepney and Ema began to cry. She no longer wears jewelry when she travels. In fact, both of us rarely wear our wedding rings for this reason.

Though incarnational leaders may sometimes be targeted for theft if they are perceived as wealthy outsiders, they are of course not the only ones who are the victims of property crimes. The urban poor themselves are also victims. Several of our neighbors have had their homes broken into and their possessions stolen. For the urban poor who live paycheck to paycheck, stolen possessions are often difficult to replace.

NATURAL & MANMADE DISASTERS. Fires, floods, and other disasters are real dangers in urban poor communities. In general, urban poor neighborhoods are located in areas where no one else wants to live. Squatter villages especially are often next to waterways, in floodplains, along railroad tracks, or by city dumps. While this protects the squatters from many land disputes, all of these locations are disasters waiting to happen.

One squatter community I have visited is all two-story wooden homes. On the first floor there are no electric outlets and only plastic furniture, because the area floods up to eight feet during storms. With every rain, residents carry the plastic furniture upstairs and turn off the breaker box for the whole house to prevent electric shock, just in case the second floor floods as well. The quality of building material used and the limited maintenance of urban poor homes means they are more susceptible to severe storm damage. During one storm, many squatters near Botocan lost their roofs, which caused massive water damage and dangerous molding. The neighboring middle-class community was unharmed by the same storm.

Fires can also be extremely devastating and are one of the more common dangers incarnational leaders in urban poor communities face. Thirty-three percent of incarnational leaders who were surveyed experienced a fire in their home or community.[31] Dave and Mini, incarnational leaders in an urban poor community in Long Beach, California, shared extensively about their experience.[32] They lived on the ground floor of a three-story apartment building. The building was built in the seventies and was originally part of a middle-class neighborhood, but the community had since changed and the building was in a state of deterioration.

As Dave returned home one day, the fire alarm went off. At first they did not pay attention because there were frequent false alarms. However, since their daughter Lily was only five months old and Dave was on crutches, they decided to take their daughter and a few important things outside. As they left, Dave heard a woman screaming from her balcony. Smoke filled her place and was pouring out from the windows. She was pregnant and panicking. It looked like she might jump from the third story, but Dave returned to his now smoke-filled apartment to get a rope. Another man retrieved a ladder and climbed onto the balcony of the second floor. The woman climbed over her own balcony rail, hung, and dropped. The man caught her and was able to take her down the ladder. She herself was unharmed, but unfortunately the stress would contribute to a miscarriage. Two others died along with the baby, and many were hospitalized.

Dave and Mini's home was totally destroyed because of smoke damage. The extent of the fire was directly related to the deteriorating condition of the building. If the building had been up to proper fire codes, the fire would not have spread throughout the apartment complex as it had. We join the poor in being vulnerable to disasters due to lack of community infrastructure.

Health

Urban poor life has its fair share of health hazards. Mildly irritating sicknesses like the common cold, pinkeye, and lice are extremely common. We regularly keep medicated eye drops and lice shampoo on hand so we can treat our conditions at first notice—before we contribute to their spread.

With their dense populations, poor water quality and access, and often inadequate healthcare, poor communities are prone to outbreaks of potentially deadly epidemics. Incarnational leaders are just as susceptible to contracting potentially deadly diseases as anyone else in the community, and may be more sensitive to certain diseases than locals with previous exposure. Tuberculosis is a common airborne disease among the urban poor in Manila. During my third year in Manila, I was sick with a fever and had night sweats so intense that I would go to sleep with a shirt on, only to have to wake up in the middle of the night to change my soaking wet shirt. Before long, my neighbors and I recognized these as symptoms of tuberculosis. A chest x-ray confirmed that I had in fact contracted the disease.

In most urban poor communities, there is reasonable nearby access to modern health care for those who are willing and able to pay. An incarnational leader might appropriately choose to seek health information and care of a higher quality and more frequently than his or her average neighbor. The incarnational leader can contribute a lot to the community's health by becoming a liaison, helping neighbors navigate the system during emergencies and offering informal health advice when needed. The cost of frequent illness is already ingrained in incarnational ministry, but prolonging illness and risking death by declining care are unnecessary costs.

The Threat of Violence

The stereotypes of poor communities are often scarier than the actual realities of day-to-day life, but violence is not a myth by any means. Communities aren't plagued by violence because the urban poor are less moral, but because any human being can be tempted to violence when faced with a lack of resources and appropriate avenues for self-expression and self-advocacy, and when they are trapped in cycles of cultural and family violence.

There are two forms of violence that both the urban poor and incarnational leaders face: external and internal. External violence is violence from outside the community. In some places, foreign and domestic military attacks are a threat. But in the Philippines and many other nations, external violence comes in the form of police brutality. In Balic-Balic, the police force terrorized the community. They would frequently come through the community to make raids and random arrests. One afternoon, they came through the community arresting every man that was not wearing a shirt, which was practically every man in the community. Anyone who resisted was beaten. Fortunately, Botocan has a much better relationship with the local police force than Balic-Balic, but we still face occasional incidents.

Internal violence is violence from within the community. This includes domestic violence, neighbors fighting, and gang warfare. Domestic violence has been the most common form of violence in both Botocan and Balic-Balic. We have ministered to many women who were beaten by their husbands, men who were beaten by their wives, and children who were beaten by their parents. One man approached us requesting marriage counseling after his wife hit him with a glass bottle in the head so hard he was hospitalized for several days.

Neighbors fighting with each other is also fairly common. It can get particularly ugly when people are drinking. Recently, a young teenager in our community was killed after flirting with another man's girlfriend at a drunken party. Sometimes these feuds happen along lines of gang affiliations. Though not every gang is as violent and murderous as the media stereotypes, incarnational leaders should avoid real or perceived allegiance to a gang in order to protect themselves, their families and ministry teams, and their churches from getting caught up in violent disputes.

It is easy to end up in the middle of a fight through no fault of your own. I know of a man who was hit in the head with a metal pipe when he unknowingly walked into the middle of a fight. He was hit so hard that he eventually needed brain surgery. I experienced my first shoot-out one evening as I was fetching water. When I was about halfway through my trips across the tracks, I was suddenly surrounded by the sound of gunshots. Another man and I ducked behind a wall. He asked me if I was bleeding. I took a moment to examine myself to make sure that I was not shot. We were both unscathed. After a minute, we ran back to the house and stayed inside. We found out later that evening that the shooters were the police. They shot the father of one of the children who sometimes came to our church during a drug raid. He was hospitalized and survived the shooting. Months later, when I spoke to the child about her dad being shot, the five-year-old acted as if it was a normal occurrence.

For women, one of the major safety concerns is the threat of sexual assault. A man in Balic-Balic used to try to grab Ema as she walked by. He also stalked her whenever she left the house, so she could never go out by herself. This is realistic to the experience of urban poor women, whose movements and decisions can be extremely restricted by the threat of violence. Moving in groups is a common strategy to help meet this threat. Ema's ordeal ended when the man was arrested for murder, which was not a comforting outcome.

We do not want to normalize violence so much that it no longer makes us flinch. A certain amount of healthy fear can help us to stick close to our neighbors and to remember to travel in pairs and groups, as we probably should anyway. However, the fear of violence can lead to defensive measures, such as locks and bars, and unnecessarily limits our movement. Fear also causes us to look at neighbors with a certain amount of suspicion. When fear dominates our thoughts and emotions, we are hindered in our ability to live meaningfully in our community and to engage the community for transformation. To some extent, we need to accept the risk of violence as a cost and learn to live within it effectively.

The Emotional Toll

Urban poor ministry is emotionally draining and demanding. Throughout our journey among the urban poor, Ema and I have experienced doubts, discouragements, failures, and frustrations that have greatly dampened our spirits. No one is exempt from experiencing emotional pain in this type of ministry.

The causes of emotional pain are plentiful. The people around us suffer greatly from all forms of injustice, personal sins, and calamities. Neighbors verbally and physically abuse their spouses and children. Even things that seemed fascinating about the community upon moving in can be sources of stress and irritation. Self-care is difficult in these urban contexts, especially for introverts. Sometimes I desperately need quiet time to process stress and heartache by myself, but I cannot find it.

Grief over death, especially preventable death, takes a huge toll on any incarnational leader. Jen, an incarnational leader in Los Angeles, experienced this when she heard nearby gunshots one afternoon, followed by a frantic banging at her door.

She opened the door to find a man from the neighborhood telling her to call 911 because somebody had been shot. The 911 dispatcher had her perform emergency first aid on the injured man to try and stop the bleeding. An ambulance arrived but did not come down the block because there was a crowd around the man. The police showed up and had the people disperse. The police made Jen stop the emergency first aid and back away. They did nothing for the man as they just waited for the ambulance to get closer. The man had been conscious when Jen was forced to stop intervening, but by the time the paramedics got there, he had died. The community was of course angered by how the police responded, rightly seeing it as another type of violence.

At dusk, the man's family began showing up. Jen met the family, and they thanked her for trying to help him. She met the man's girlfriend, who shared about his life. He was in a gang, and she had threatened to break up with him if he did not change. That morning, he had called her and said he was ready to leave his old life. As he rode his bike away from the pay phone, a car pulled up and asked him who he ran with. He flashed his gang sign and was immediately shot. His girlfriend was devastated; he was so close to getting out. While we can say with confidence that God was present as Jen entered into grief with the man's girlfriend and family, the trauma of being forced to watch him die still haunts Jen and the community.[33]

One particularly painful time in our own ministry was Carmela's death. Carmela was a nine-year-old neighbor in Balic-Balic who used to come over all the time to practice reading. She was a bubbly girl, who was full of life and energy. One day in November, Carmela had a fever. A few days later, the fever worsened and she grew weak. By the time her parents took her to the hospital, it was too late. She died later that night. At Carmela's funeral, we discovered that the funeral home was out of child-sized caskets. Lying in a casket that was way too big for her made her body look even smaller. Seeing a child die is extremely heart-wrenching, and it does not become easier over time. Carmela was the first death we experienced of someone we were close to. It will certainly not be the last.

Poverty is not for the faint of heart. No one begins their journey among the urban poor thinking they will eventually need years of counseling and healing prayer to recover. I am always saddened when I meet with former urban poor workers who left urban poor ministry broken, bitter, and frustrated. None of this is meant to discourage sensitive readers from following their call, but it is meant to help prepare them. God can call the sensitive, the anxious, and the depressed, but in my experience, he will call them to seek mental and emotional health as part of their ministry preparation and maintenance. Just as with physical health, getting good mental health care is of great benefit to your community as well.

Emotional co-suffering with one's neighbors can be a source of deep connection, empathy, and desire to be mutually supportive. It is not something to be either avoided or indulged in. Ultimately, any incarnational leader will need to turn the community's sufferings over to God, laying them at the foot of the cross in prayer.

Spiritual Distress

Certain communities are more conducive to spiritual growth than others. Though we will discuss the many spiritual riches that an urban poor minister can experience, there is no denying that life among the urban poor can be a spiritual challenge.

HOPELESSNESS. The words of Agur as recorded in Proverbs give insight regarding the impact our social situation has on our spiritual life. "Two things I ask of you; deny them not to me before I die: Remove far from me falsehood and lying; give me neither poverty nor riches; feed me with the food that is needful for me, lest I be full and deny you and say, 'Who is the LORD?' or lest I be poor and steal and profane the name of my God."[34] Both poverty and riches can hinder our walk with God. This is true for individuals as well as for communities. When a community is destitute economically and the residents are in despair, there is a hopelessness that creeps in and hinders both the spread of the gospel and spiritual growth. In survival mode, the draw to sin can be overwhelming and can even become part of the culture.

However, the passage points out that material comfort is also a threat to spiritual health. The illusion of self-sufficiency comes with the temptation to forget God. The spiritual dangers associated with wealthy communities are much greater than the spiritual dangers for a destitute community. The seduction of wealth is so subtle that we can be fully engrossed in the worship of shopping and possessions without giving Jesus a second thought. By following Jesus without regard to possessions or power, we are able to experience the joy of truly living by faith. This is discipleship that recognizes the spiritual dangers of materialism and seeks to love God more than money.

TEMPTATION. Whatever our spiritual weakness may be, we will face temptation in an urban poor community. On numerous occasions, I have seen more of my female neighbors than I should have. Once, during a Bible study in a multi-story squatter home, the host's daughter, who was in her early twenties, returned home and climbed the ladder to the third floor. From where I was sitting I could see into the third floor. A few minutes later, I happened to look up at exactly the same moment she was changing her clothes. Embarrassed, I looked down immediately.

On another occasion, as I fetched water from a neighbor's faucet in the early morning, I noticed a pornographic newspaper someone dropped right in front of my door. During each trip back from my neighbor's faucet to the drum in my bathroom I had to pass the newspaper. I finally got a scoop of water, poured it on the newspaper, stood on the newspaper, and twisted my feet to turn it into mush. An urban leader must accept that he or she will face temptation and the tension and discomfort that comes with it.

SPIRITUAL RESISTANCE. Spiritual attacks are also common for incarnational leaders. These attacks can take many different forms. Our experience of hosting short-term teams in a squatter community has been that at least one person has been troubled by nightmares on almost every team. People who are sensitive to spiritual resistance may feel this as a great cost. However, it can also be a sign that there is something worthwhile at stake in your decision to move.

Michele in Oakland, California faced spiritual attacks soon after her arrival.[35] It started with community violence, and then the nightmares followed. The third day she was there, she heard gunfire outside her home and a stray bullet came through the wall. Not long after that, a mini bomb was set off in front of her house, which shook the glass windows and set off everyone's car alarms. Her housemates, who had been there longer, noticed community violence intensified when their ministry started. As for the nightmares, they were much worse than simply bad dreams. She woke up late one night with a bad feeling, so she started praying and singing worship songs. She had been given a new bottle of anointing oil earlier that day, but when she looked at it again it was almost empty. A voice in her head said, "See, your God is not a God of abundance, but of scarcity, and he cannot protect you from me."

At that point she knew she really needed to seek God in prayer and began reading through Psalm 118. The next day she talked with her spiritual director, who told her that she also woke up and felt the urge to pray and read Psalm 118. It was a particularly difficult year, but through prayer the situation has begun to improve. While a minister might experience spiritual resistance anywhere, it can be a heavy burden when added to an already difficult context. Trusting God to respond and push through the resistance with you can help.

Status and Acceptance

Incarnational leaders are not winning the game that the world is playing. There may always be some part of us that wants visible achievement, respect, and the understanding of our families, and we have to mourn those things as very real costs of moving in with the urban poor.

Turning your back on materialism and consumerism to live among the urban poor is about as counter-cultural as you can get, and that can cause inherent discomfort in your relation-ships with middle-class people. It is hard to find affirmation from others who do not have a category for your way of living.

It is not uncommon for others to feel self-conscious or defensive about their own life choices because you have made drastically different ones. It would be wrong and unhelpful to look down on our middle-class peers or assume that this is happening whenever a disagreement arises, but we do have to release our aspirations of being likeable and impressive to our peers.

The Bible is full of stories of the faithful who were counter-cultural, and thus not very well liked. After Amos prophesied in the Northern Kingdom, the priests told him to go home and never return: "And Amaziah (the priest of Bethel) said to Amos, 'O seer, go, flee away to the land of Judah, and eat bread there, and prophesy there, but never again prophesy at Bethel, for it is the king's sanctuary, and it is a temple of the Kingdom.'"[36] Amos's message was not well-received, and he was challenged because of it. Jeremiah's message also raised opposition. He was beaten and put in the stocks for his ministry.[37]

In addition, your loved ones may be genuinely concerned about all of these costs and dangers, and try to dissuade you from this path. In the experience of my colleagues, single women have been particularly pressured by their mothers for this reason. If you determine that you shouldn't be persuaded by them, they may be genuinely hurt. It is important to handle those situations sensitively and try to maintain as much of a relationship as possible.

Over the years, I have been consistently pressured to seek a normal middle-class life. I have found that the longer I live among the urban poor, the more I am asked by friends and family when I am going to move out. After we had Zach, many simply assumed we would transfer to a middle-class community. I have been fortunate in that, for the most part, my family has been supportive of our decision. Some incarnational leaders face relentless opposition to their decision to live among the urban poor.

I usually deal with opposition by focusing on the positive aspects of urban poor life. With my parents, I stress the benefits of urban poor life, such as the large number of playmates Zach and Ezra have and the invaluable experience they have been given. This realization has helped them to accept the fact that their son and grandsons are fully at home in a majority-world squatter community.

Though there will always be personal disagreements between neighbors, widespread rejection from the urban poor themselves should definitely give pause to a leader. We might need to avoid detection by a government that is hostile to religion and ministry, and we might need to risk violence from the police or corrupt local governments, but our relationship to the urban poor is the very heart of our ministry. If the community members themselves are avoiding, ostracizing, or undermining you, it is time to stop, listen, and redirect. You may be experiencing rejection as a perceived religious authority figure. Starting again with peer relationships is crucial. You may have lost the trust of the community because of bad experiences with (or prejudices against) religion, the middle class, leaders of your gender or nationality, or an institution that you have collaborated with. Sincerely addressing these concerns would be the next step in this case.

In some Christian circles, being an incarnational leader does come with a high status. Leaders among the urban poor can even be idealized as saints, both by the urban poor and by their middle-class peers. Though it is tempting to embrace and even flaunt this new status, it is crucial to instead reject the inappropriate praise of others and hold on to a genuine humility. We must always convey the truth that we are peers to our neighbors, not experts, not morally superior. If we are offered leadership positons or awards simply for living incarnationally, we must be willing to decline them in most cases. This is not a cost imposed upon us, but a cost that we must constantly remind ourselves to pay.

Conclusion

There are certainly many costs to living in an urban poor community. Time, sleep, cleanliness, material security, safety, mental and physical health, and status all need to be surrendered to God as you follow his call into this life. Romanticizing the urban poor life is a mistake that leads to disillusionment and burnout among many leaders. Recognizing now what will be most difficult about your experience can help you to prayerfully prepare and have realistic expectations about the nature of your ministry.

[29] Luke 12:16-34
[30] See Appendix B.
[31] See Appendix B.
[32] Interview with Dave Palmer, July 28, 2011. Charlottesville, VA.
[33] Interview with Jen Blue, August 17, 2011. Los Angeles, CA.
[34] Prov. 30:7-9
[35] Interview with Michele Blanton Cho, August 4, 2011. Los Angeles, CA.
[36] Amos 7:12-13
[37] Jer. 20:2

5

YOUR ROLE AS NEIGHBOR

WHILE INCARNATIONAL LEADERS can have an array of specific ministries, our role as a neighbor is central and foundational to all of them. A dictionary might tell you that a neighbor is anyone who shares a property line or a zip code. But in chapter 10 of the Gospel of Luke, Jesus gives a different definition.[38]

An expert in the Law tested Jesus with a question about how to inherit eternal life. In response, Jesus asked, "What is written in the Law? How do you read it?" The expert in the Law stated the standard answer from Jewish Scripture: to love God and love your neighbor as yourself. When Jesus affirmed this answer, the expert in the Law went on to ask, "And who is my neighbor?" Jesus responded, as he often did, with a parable.

In this story, an unnamed man is beaten, robbed, and left for dead. Two religious men pass by and do nothing, but a Samaritan man comes to the man's aid and cares for him at great personal cost. At the time, Jews had significant racial and religious prejudices toward this neighboring group, and the shock of this story is missed if we overlook the fact that Jesus portrays a Samaritan as the hero of the story. Jesus pointedly undermines this form of socially constructed hierarchy and racism. In conclusion to the parable, Jesus asked the expert in the Law which character "proved to be a neighbor," to which the expert responded, "The one who showed him mercy."

The Samaritan became a neighbor when he got off his donkey to come to the aid of the man. While we would like to limit our love to those people who we would consider our peers, Jesus instead puts the duty of neighborliness onto all of those who would follow Him. Kristin Jack of SERVANTS echoes the meaning of Christ's command to "go and do likewise" when she says, "If you see someone hurting, get your body there."[39] This, Jack says, is what it means to be incarnational.

Jesus' affirmation of the Old Testament command to love our neighbors "as ourselves" provides further instruction to the incarnational leader. Love for self means that we desire to grow in our relationship with God, as well as good employment, safe housing, proper nutrition, and health care for ourselves. Loving our neighbor in this way means desiring these same things for them. The choice to live among the urban poor must include the choice to seek to be a good neighbor in our community by intentionally contributing to its well-being, while not despising our own.

The following are some practical ways in which we can love our neighbors in the community where we live.

Sharing Possessions

Our first urban poor house as a married couple had two stories. Downstairs was a bathroom and a kitchen sink, which really only served as a drain because we did not have running water. There was also a small stove and some kitchen utensils. Upstairs was our bedroom. That was it. Viv Grigg, our mentor and a pioneer of urban poor ministry, usually challenges incarnational leaders to live simply, but when he came to visit us, he actually counseled that we needed to make our home welcoming so that we could host guests. Kids might not mind sitting on the floor, but we really should have chairs for adults. Ema took Viv's counsel to heart and bought a small couch and chairs the next day. Ever since then, we have tried to balance our core values of simplicity and generosity.

Generosity is an important aspect of our faith. When living among the urban poor, we have daily opportunities to share possessions. This can be as simple as letting students borrow a dictionary for their homework, or it can be giving food, medicine, or occasionally small amounts of cash for emergencies. It also involves graciously accepting the generosity of others on the many occasions that they share with us.

Hospitality is a form of generosity that is central to our ministry in our community. Inviting neighbors over for meals is not only a great way to share food with those who do not have enough, it is also an excellent way to develop relationships. On one occasion, we personally experienced something similar to Jesus' parable of the great banquet. In Jesus' parable, a rich man hosted a dinner, but the ones invited did not come, so the poor were invited.[40] Ema cooked way too much food for a church planning meeting and several leaders were not able to attend. We ended up having a spontaneous communal meal with kids from our community after the meeting.

The sharing of food is reciprocal: we host our neighbors for meals and keep snacks on hand for hungry kids, and they often bring us excess crops and cook meals for us on special occasions. One neighbor visited his wife's family over the weekend and brought back a surplus of bananas. He insisted that I take a bag of bananas home with me. The man who lives above us brought a bag of green mangos he picked after work to share with us. Some of the children and youth were hanging out in our house at the time, so we were all able to enjoy the mangos together. I believe God is pleased when he sees people living in community, enjoying and sharing what they have with one another.

There are certain times, however, when it is more loving not to give. Shortly after we moved into our new home in Balic-Balic, our neighbor An came to our home in tears about a major financial crisis in her family. We gave the money she requested, but the next day she came with the same request. We gave again, but more reluctantly. When she came again on the third day, we told her that we would not keep giving her money each day. We later found out that she was doing the same thing to others in the community. We soon discovered An's family would live extravagantly for a few days after she received her paycheck and then be out of money until the next paycheck. Borrowing money with no intention of paying it back became the means of supporting her family's unhealthy spending habits. We chose not to continue to give to An and instead encouraged her to be more responsible with money.

We must correct the assumption that all of the problems of the urban poor can be solved with money, and generosity with possessions should be distinguished from relief. While generosity requires human relationships, relief is mechanically-conducted temporary emergency assistance—a gravitational flow of goods from those who have to those who need. A lifestyle of neighborly, reciprocal sharing will help incarnational leaders to be disassociated from the position of detached wealth and power that is usually given to those who dole out money and free goods in this way.

One way we have practiced reciprocal generosity is through limiting the tools that we own for ourselves. I have not purchased a hammer, mainly because I rarely use one. On those occasions when I need one, my neighbor is delighted not only to lend the hammer, but to help fix what is broken.

Sharing Services

Much of what incarnational leaders can share with urban poor neighbors (and vice versa) are not actual possessions. The sharing of skills, knowledge, and connections are very practical ways to help. The list of ways for neighbors to serve each other is limitless.

Those with specialized training can have powerful ministries among the urban poor. Ema is a trained counselor, and she has been able to provide free counseling services to many of our neighbors. One caution is that trained professionals should be the only ones who attempt to provide medical services, counseling, and technical assistance. Attempting to do counseling or rewire a house without training may cause more harm than good.

Incarnational leaders without medical training can still help neighbors by serving as gatekeepers to connect the urban poor with caring professionals. Juday, a young girl in our community with whom Ema has become friends, kept coming over asking for pain relievers because she had a bad toothache. We contacted Doctor Lisa, a dentist who is a member of the middle-class church that we are partnered with, and she agreed to treat Juday. I walked Juday to Lisa's nearby home, bringing the standard fee for care. Lisa greeted us with a smile and treated Juday free of charge. Doctor Lisa and a colleague later came to Botocan one Saturday afternoon to provide free dental services. They not only provided their time, but also paid for anesthesia and other medication out of their own pockets.

Sharing services is also reciprocal. Each summer we host internship teams from the United States. Americans tend to be hard on things. We have had all sorts of random things broken, from kitchen sinks to doors. These setbacks always provide opportunities to seek the help of our neighbors. When our church's DVD player broke, I took it to Ariel, a neighbor who fixes electronics from his home. Within about twenty minutes it was up and running again.

Sharing Space

The homes of incarnational leaders can be of service to the community in multiple ways. The leader can host Bible studies and prayer groups, as well as purely social events such as meals and full-blown parties. One reason for keeping our home simple is so that anyone in the community will feel comfortable and not self-conscious when they visit it.

There are also smaller creative ways to share your space with the community. Ema has shared space in our refrigerator, allowing neighbors to store food. On multiple occasions, different neighbors have asked us to keep meat for them. The children will ask us to put drinks in our freezer for a short time to chill. We also have neighbors stop by and ask to sit and chat in our kitchen over a cold glass of water.

An incarnational leader might also have an opportunity to practice a much bigger application of sharing space by taking in a houseguest on occasion. My friend and fellow incarnational leader from Bangkok, Michelle, shares her experience of inviting one of her neighbors to live with her.

> Our neighbor, Areva, was in a really bad living situation. Areva was only seventeen years old, but she was already selling drugs and addicted. Her boyfriend was in jail, and she had just given birth to her first child. She did

not know how to take care of her baby and would yell and scream at her infant.

We knew in order to change the course of her life, Areva needed a safe environment away from the drugs, so we decided to take her in. In the beginning, it was extremely stressful. She did not have money for diapers, so the baby would pee everywhere. Our place turned into a dump quickly. I would come home after a long, tiring day and have to clean for two hours because the house smelled.

Over time we began to see improvements. After observing how we interacted with the baby, Areva began to learn how to as well. She grew spiritually during her stay with us. She did not do personal devotions, but would do communal devotions. Our other neighbors once told us we were crazy for bringing her in. Now they comment on how much she has changed.

Eventually the church members remodeled Areva's home so that it was livable. She partnered with another church member to run a restaurant from the home. We still continually follow up with Areva since we live in the same community, and I am able to see her all the time. Of course, she still struggles and is far from perfect, particularly when it comes to handling money, but there is a definite shift in her life.

Areva is not the only one whose life has been transformed. Before, the tendency was to focus on our own lives. After welcoming Areva into our home, our focus shifted to how we could help her grow. This helped produce patience, because we had to learn to allow her to change slowly. Areva feels blessed to be in church and has grown to understand God's acceptance of her. As a church community, we have all gained a greater appreciation for our relationship with God and for our church.[41]

Taking in a houseguest or a longer-term roommate is a big decision, and a leader may sometimes correctly determine that boundaries should be set to maintain his or her family's space. However, I would challenge leaders to be open to a prayerful discernment process if a situation such as Areva's arises in the life of a friend from the community.

As incarnational leaders, our space is not strictly our own, but is an asset that we can offer to the community.

Modeling a Life of Purpose

In urban poor communities, it is not uncommon for a certain hopelessness to settle into the local culture. Without judging our neighbors, we can model a different way of living that is purposefully working toward the Kingdom.

Urban poor children and youth often have busy and worn-out parents, and the presence of a caring role model who makes countercultural decisions can make a big difference. They can demonstrate the benefits of choosing to go to school or work, even though it is more enjoyable to stay home playing video games. They can also model healthy spending habits that include limiting impulse buying, especially buying junk food, which causes a nutritional nightmare in our community as well. We also choose not to drink alcohol for a similar reason—not because alcohol is always inappropriate, but because it often plays a negative role in our community. We want to model an option for living that does not depend on alcohol to have a good time or cope with stress.

None of this amounts to criticizing neighbors or demanding that they change. We need to be humble about the fact that our errors are also on display for our neighbors as well. By being human and being vulnerable with our own flaws, we can have honest peer conversations with our neighbors about the way sin—both ours and theirs—plays out to negatively affect our families. We can begin to walk toward more purposeful lives alongside our neighbors.

Peacemaking

In many communities, the role of peacemaker is countercultural. The general (and understandable) response to community violence is self-protection through avoidance. The role of peacemaker means becoming actively involved in conflict with the intention of elevating it toward the good.

A ministry to street children sponsored a week-long trip to a beach resort for the youth of our community. We took fifty-six youth from Botocan, and twenty-seven street children from other parts of Manila joined us. Some of these youth had very rough backgrounds, including drug use, prostitution, and gang involvement. The lowest point in the camp was the dinner on the evening of our evangelistic program. One young man stole a knife from the kitchen, plotting revenge against some older boys because they played a joke on him while he was sleeping. After disarming the youth, we proceeded with the evangelistic program. I was very distracted by the evident tension; I actually prayed that no one would get killed during the camp. Ultimately, we discovered that fourteen youth, including several gang members, were involved in the brewing conflict. The two groups involved were separated and given space to vent their anger. We discovered the nature of the conflict and had them agree to meet to discuss a truce.

After setting the rules for the meeting, Ema facilitated the conflict resolution. At one point, one of them stood up and took off his shirt like he was going to fight, but Ema was able to maintain control and have them talk through the issues. That meeting changed the whole atmosphere of the camp. On the last evening of camp, one of the gang leaders who was influential in the negotiation process even called me over so we could have our picture taken together.

The role of peacemaker can be very serious—and potentially deadly. Incarnational leaders will see acts of violence in their communities and have to make split-second decisions about what to do. I know one incarnational leader who acted as peacemaker by throwing himself on top of a man who was being beaten so the kicks and punches would hit him and not the man. Fortunately, this act shamed the group so much that they stopped beating him and left. However, acting as peacemaker does not always involve dramatic negotiations or hospital visits. In fact, it rarely does. Our usual role as peacemaker is either breaking up fights between young kids or talking through issues with friends and family members who are fighting.

There is no single way to be a peacemaker in your community, and there is no single right response in all situations. Incarnational leaders need to trust the Holy Spirit to give wisdom when violence arises and a peacemaker is needed.

Prayer

Praying for our neighborhood is central to engaging the community for transformation. God works through intercessory prayer not only to transform communities, but also to transform the hearts of the intercessors. I have become emotionally connected to Botocan through praying for the community. As I develop stronger relationships with my neighbors, I find myself continually praying for them.

Michele, an incarnational leader in Oakland, regularly prays for her neighborhood. During prayer walks, Michele and her team would offer to pray for their neighbors who were out. They would also invite them to weekly prayer meetings. At one of these meetings, they prayed for a neighbor whose relative was murdered and whose house was being threatened with foreclosure. This neighbor was afraid the killer would be found not guilty and attempt to get revenge on her family for testifying against him. After the prayer time, the bank provided an emergency loan so she could keep her home, and the killer was found guilty. This helped open doors for further ministry in the community, which in turn paved the way for future transformations.[42]

God also uses prayer to soften the hearts of incarnational leaders toward their neighbors. Often, the natural tendency is to slowly become hard-hearted toward neighbors as the stress of life with them compiles. Intercession helps incarnational leaders to continually have compassion for their neighbors without becoming overburdened by their problems. Prayer for local criminals prevents incarnational leaders from becoming angry and wanting revenge. In Michele's Oakland community, an ex-gang member who became involved in a local church was trying to leave his gang. In response, he was shot six times by the gang members. Miraculously, he survived the shooting. They originally prayed for his recovery, then shifted their prayers toward his attackers. The act of praying for the shooters helped the community of believers see the humanity in the gang members. They still wanted justice, but not vengeance.

Several female incarnational leaders in Oakland became friends with Juan, a male neighbor. It is often tricky ministering across gender lines, and his girlfriend, Brenda, became upset about other women befriending her boyfriend. She actually cussed them out and threatened them. Juan was excited to join a men's Bible study, but Brenda did not want the women to communicate with him. After months of prayer for both Juan and his girlfriend, the incarnational leaders learned that Brenda was pregnant. They decided to have a baby shower for her, and the gesture softened her heart and reconciled their relationship. The baby shower opened doors for ministry throughout the apartment complex.[43]

The incarnational leaders could have responded to the initial threats by simply avoiding Brenda. They could have justified their hard hearts toward her by claiming that she was resistant to the gospel. However, by regularly praying for her, their own hearts were softened enough that they wanted to host a baby shower for her.

Conclusion

Becoming a neighbor means much more than just moving in. Following the Samaritan character in Christ's parable, we become neighbors when we reach out across cultural boundaries to love our urban poor neighbors as ourselves. This means sharing possessions, services, and space, as well as offering an example of a life shaped by purpose in Christ, making peace in violent spaces, and praying continually for our communities. Neighborliness is something we carry with us into our communities.

---

[38] Luke 10:26-39
[39] Kristin Jack, ed. *The Sound of Worlds Colliding: Stories of Radical Discipleship from Servants to Asia's Urban Poor* (Phnom Penh, Cambodia: Hawaii Printing House, 2009), 42.
[40] Luke 14:15-24
[41] Interview with Michelle Kao, July 21, 2011. Charlottesville, VA.
[42] Interview with Michele Blanton Cho.
[43] Ibid.

6

YOUR ROLE AS MINISTER

DEPENDING ON YOUR CALL and journey, you may or may not have an official church role in your community. However, since the church body is such a powerful means of Kingdom transformation, it is important for every incarnational leader to minister through the activities and initiatives of the local church, and to support official church workers in their efforts to minister incarnationally.

In *Building a People of Power*, urban theologian and community organizer Robert Linthicum offers a church-based practice of incarnational ministry which partners with the community for transformation. He believes that incarnational ministry does not merely involve individual Christians, but an entire community of believers as members of a church that is physically located in an urban poor community. Linthicum writes, "When a church seeks to minister with its community, it seeks to incarnate itself in that community."[44] A church with its community is one that "enters into the life of that community and becomes partners with the community in addressing that community's needs."[45] We should seek to be involved in or even help to initiate churches with an incarnational mindset.

Church Planting

In some communities, there are either no churches, or not enough churches to serve the needs of the community. In these situations the incarnational leader may become part of an initiative to begin a congregation. As is almost always the case, our partnership with a better established church has been an asset to Botocan Bible Christian Fellowship (BBCF). In fact, the partner church is some-times even the parent church: growing churches often send some of their members to begin new churches in their communities.

This usually happens in a few phases. The first phase, building relationships with neighbors, was discussed in the previous chapter. In Botocan, it was those initial relationships that opened the door for the first Bible study group, which eventually led to launching our church as a regular weekly worship group. Church planting is the main focus of our current ministry. Every community is different, and in some communities a different approach may be more appropriate.

Community empowerment must be the central question when deciding if and how to begin a church. Immediately after moving into Botocan, neighbors began asking us what we were giving away. They were accustomed to being the passive recipients of free goods and services, rather than active members and leaders of church programs. We deliberately chose to root our church in evangelism and discipleship before beginning any social programs because we wanted to break this cycle, with programs coming out of collaboration and true relationship.

The ministry team of BBCF has included a variety of incar-national leaders, both local and relocated, since we first planted the church in 2009. When the church was started, the ministry team consisted of three people who lived in the community and three commuters. Currently, the entire leadership team lives in the community. As BBCF has grown, several other indigenous leaders have begun to take leadership responsibilities. This transition is integral to successful, healthy church planting. Without community ownership, the church maintains power imbalances that are not part of the Kingdom.

During summer vacation, when customized temporary tattoos are in fashion, many of the youth in church now etch "Jesus" or "BBCF" (the church initials) on their arms or legs to show their membership. Some of the young women at church followed through on their own idea to set up a fingernail art booth at the community fiesta as a way to share about Jesus and invite people to our church. Because there is a sense of community ownership, members do not need my prodding or permission to get involved and take on leadership roles. If anything, I just help when I'm asked to do so.

Evangelism

We have daily opportunities to show and tell others about Jesus. We should not have to schedule an evangelistic program or have a tract distribution day in order to share the good news of our faith. Many of us are familiar with Jesus' Great Commission in Matthew 28:

> And Jesus came and said to them, "All authority in heaven and on earth has been given to me. Go there-fore and make disciples of all nations, baptizing them in the name of the Father and of the Son and of the Holy Spirit, teaching them to observe all that I have commanded you. And behold, I am with you always, to the end of the age."[46]

This central calling means we testify to who Jesus is with our whole lives, and are always ready to talk about him. Everyone deserves a chance to hear about Jesus, especially the people that are around us in our everyday lives.

In my morning walks with Zach and Ezra, I will stop and talk with people. Community residents know we started a new church, and I routinely get the opportunity to talk with them about Jesus and our church. I sometimes ask if I can pray for people, even those I do not know well. These are natural ways I have been able to verbally proclaim Jesus to my neighbors.

A man who lives above us had been sober for several months, but suddenly went back to drinking. Ema asked him why, and he shared a story about a woman who he liked, but who was not interested in him. In the aftermath, drinking was his only source of comfort. Ema told him true comfort, the kind he was looking for, is found in God. Nodding in agreement, he began to cry. This man would never sit through a Bible study, or a church service, but because our ministry goes with us into the community, Ema and I have both had the opportunity to share about Jesus with him. We continue to pray that he would find hope in a new relationship with Christ, and we are excited at the possibility of being a part of that renewal.

As a church, we evangelize not usually as a program, but by encouraging each other to find and embrace opportunities like this. Other churches may engage in evangelism differently, but I believe that every church should hold it as a shared value.

Discipleship

Discipleship means walking alongside people in relationships that are geared toward supporting their faith. It means encouraging

86

people to leave harmful sins behind, pray, and adopt spiritual disciplines to grow their own relationships with Jesus. The ministry of discipleship is how we finish carrying out Jesus' Great Commission.

Incarnational ministry makes true discipleship possible. It ensures discipleship encompasses every dimension of Christian life. By being neighbors with those we are helping grow in discipleship, we see them and they see us in the normal context of life. Yes, we have church programs such as a worship service, prayer meeting, and small group Bible studies, but the important part of the discipleship process is not the few hours per week in these programs. Discipleship also includes hanging out together at the basketball court with the intention of encouraging others in their walk with God. It is informally answering questions that someone has about God or the Bible, and finding ways to remind them that you and God both care about them.

There is certainly more than one right way to do discipleship among the urban poor. Even within the same community, discipleship will look different for people with different personalities as well as for those who are at various stages in their walk with God. Over the years, I have used a variety of approaches. When I was working with JR from Balic-Balic, we would read the same sections of Scripture throughout the week for our personal devotions. We would then meet each week to discuss passages that stood out to us, questions we had, and what God was teaching us. With others I would prepare questions on the text that we were studying and we would discuss the passage together.

Communal discipleship, as opposed to individual, should be practiced whenever possible. Traditionally, Filipinos are group-oriented people. Because of this, we decided to try a communal style discipleship that moved beyond small groups. As a church, we began to have group devotions every morning. During the school year, a few believers from Botocan would gather each morning for communal devotions.

Bible studies are ideally a form of group discipleship. In BBCF, the main Bible study method we use is what we call Community Bible Interpretation. This is a contextualized approach to biblical interpretation among the urban poor in Manila. It is based on how information is shared among peers. Adapting this to biblical interpretation, the Bible studies we hold at BBCF are not lecture style, but discussions where the passage is explored as a group. As a leader, I no longer have to guess which parts of the text speak to them, as this becomes clear during our discussion of the passage. Before we close the discussion, everyone is given a chance to share an application from the text.

In every form of discipleship, an important priority is addressing the distorted self-image of the poor by focusing on their value in God's eyes. The poor are often ashamed and humiliated by their poverty, and can come to believe that they are inferior to others. By encouraging our neighbors to grow in their understanding of and relationship with God, we also try to help our neighbors see themselves as God sees them.

Although many urban poor can read, there may be some who are non-literate. Reading is not necessary to grow spiritually, especially with today's audio Bibles and recorded sermons, dramas, and songs. In most cases, though, an urban poor follower of Jesus who is non-literate should be taught how to read as part of his or her discipleship. Knowing how to read is a form of empowerment, not only because it allows them to read and study the Bible for themselves, but because it opens up many positive opportunities in the rest of life as well.

Leadership Development

Leadership development in urban poor communities should not be viewed as a start-from-scratch project. Leaders already exist in the community. We simply need to find these leaders with God's guidance and help them continue to grow in Christ and in their leadership ability. By being meaningfully present in the community, incarnational leaders are able to better identify its leaders.

An important part of leadership development is helping church members exercise their gifts and skills by providing opportunities to lead. BBCF sponsors formal leadership training seminars, but it is even more important for members to learn through experience. Churches that encourage all of their members to be involved in a wide variety of ministries and have on-the-job-training are able to develop local leaders.

One of the strengths of BBCF is that we intentionally give leadership responsibility to as many people as possible. This has resulted in a strong sense of community ownership of the church. By now, the members often plan and run whole programs on their own. One year, the youth in our church put together a skit for our partner church's Christmas party. This gave the youth a forum from which they were able to grow as leaders.

Handing over leadership, especially to those who are just learning how to lead, can be messy. The incarnational leader needs to be prepared for the mistakes that new leaders need to make in order to grow. I have had to lead several spontaneous Bible studies because one of our potential leaders backed out at the last minute. On occasion we've had to postpone programs because they were not ready. Being given the opportunity to fail is a key part of any growing leader's learning process. Though it can be messy and even costly, it is part of our goal of empowering our communities.

Integral Mission

Integral mission is the natural blending of evangelism and social action. Becoming a community member and a ministry leader demands that incarnational leaders sometimes intervene in larger community issues. It is a frustrating experience to have a beloved church member tell you, "I can't afford to be a Christian anymore. I've stopped selling drugs, and now I have no more income. My family is blaming Christianity for the hardship they are now facing. I have to go back to my old life in order to survive." Urban poor followers of Jesus who used to be involved in criminal activity do need discipleship that focuses on Jesus being greater than money or acceptance. However, the church also has a responsibility to help open doors for alternative jobs. Community development is a way in which churches can become involved in addressing larger social issues in the community.

Community organizing toward group action on social issues is a key avenue to bring about community transformation. Robert Linthicum writes, "Doing community organizing is always doing ministry 'with' a community, never 'to' or 'in' a community."[47] This method stresses humility and acknowledges the people within a community are the ones who best know their own needs. Truly being with a community requires a mindset of being in partnership with locals and putting your space and social capital at the service of their initiatives.

Community organizing is much more than simply protesting against government agencies or businesses. The ideal outcome of an action initiated by community organizing is to get government agencies and businesses to join the community's side and to work together for transformation. As leaders of church institutions, incarnational ministers often have the cultural capital needed to need engage government and businesses in the community's initiatives for long-term, sustainable community transformation. Admittedly, this does not always happen, but it is still something to strive for. In some cases, destructive businesses and politicians need to be replaced by healthier influences.

Specialized Ministries

Over my years working with the urban poor, I've come to realize that the urban poor are not a monolithic grouping; they belong to a huge array of groups and cultures. Some urban poor groups include students, street children, single adults, families, youth gangs, prostitutes, drug addicts, people with special needs, or employment-specific groups. These groups often develop their own subculture within the mainstream culture.

In a community-focused ministry, incarnational leaders should attempt to reach all of the groups represented within the community, not just one specific group or the imaginary "average" resident. Tutoring, children's clubs, musicians' groups, sports events, and recovery programs are examples of programs that are tailored to meet the needs and passions of specific groups.

Sometimes, specialized ministries can be a way of beginning a new fellowship. A church planter once told me that "you can't plant a church if you begin with a children's ministry." I'm not sure where he worked as a church planter, but I am guessing it was not among the urban poor! In my experience, nothing could be further from the truth. Faith Gospel Community (FGC), a sister church in Botocan, originally started as a children's Sunday school. As the kids grew up they started a youth ministry. By that time, a focused effort on reaching the parents had begun to bear fruit and a church was planted. Many of those original Sunday school attendees are now the church leaders. Contrary to what this particular church planter said, reaching children can lead to whole families coming to faith in Jesus, and the same can be said for the members of any other specialized group.

While we are able to reach many groups from a community-based ministry, a problem we encounter is that we do not have the specialization that is often needed to meet every need. For example, it is not easy to have gang members attending church. Because most of our leaders are not part of gang culture, it is difficult to understand and address their unique needs. For example, when we take the youth to a nearby university to exercise on their sports field, we have to pass another gang's turf. The gang members from our community do not dare come with us. If our church had the capacity for a full-time gang member ministry, it could tailor events that were always accessible to these individuals.

Sometimes, a church will want to partner with an external organization to meet the needs of a specialized group. If the organization is not based in the community, everyone involved will need to be extremely intentional in order to make sure its implementation ends up being incarnational. One way to do this is to make sure that the local church (or individual incarnational leader) retains the decision-making and implementing roles as the program is carried out. The specialized ministry partner would act as a grant writer and consultant, providing the resources and expertise needed to engage the group. This avoids the common problem that specialized ministries often dictate rules and policies without actually understanding the dynamics of the local group.

However, a value for the community's autonomy generally means limiting dependence on external funding. We are in a very real sense beholden to those who write our paychecks, and it is my experience that far too many organizations use the golden rule—namely, "We have the gold, so we make the rules." A children's aid organization once partnered with an urban poor church in

Manila. The church provided workers and the specialized ministry provided the finances. Problems began when the pastor and the nonprofit disagreed on their vision for the direction of the local church. It was inappropriate for the organization to influence the direction of the entire church at all, but since the church leaders worked for the organization, their loyalties shifted from the church to their employer. Eventually, a split happened and those employed by the specialized ministry started their own church.

We need to recognize that any funding source will be influential in a ministry. Sometimes, having smaller programming for specialized groups within the community's own capacity is really the better decision for the long-term sustainability of the ministry.

Conclusion

Engaging an urban poor community for transformation can take numerous forms, so one person's task list may not look like another's. If you have a full-time job or school schedule, you may not be a part of official church leadership. However, if you are ministering incarnationally in any capacity, it is important to recognize and support the important role that church and para-church ministry can take as we accompany communities in their own transformation. Church planting, evangelism, discipleship, leadership development, integral mission, and specialized ministries are just some of the ways that a church can meaningfully engage many members of the community in their faith and day-to-day lives.

---

[44] Robert C. Linthicum, *Building a People of Power: Equipping Churches to Transform Their Communities* (Waynesboro, GA: Authentic Media, 2006), 279.
[45] Ibid.
[46] Matt. 28:19-20.
[47] Linthicum, *Building a People of Power*, 292.

7

YOUR CHANGING FAMILY ROLE

WHEN YOU MAKE A TRANSITION to a life of incarnational ministry among the urban poor, your family will be affected. This is true of everyone, at every life stage, and so it is always a part of the discernment of our calling. Some people, such as a spouse or the caretaker of a minister with a disability, will usually have a sort of veto power within our discernment process, while other loved ones should be thoughtfully accommodated whenever it does not lead to compromise. In any case, the care and concern of our families should be honored as much as possible.

Family dynamics may also influence seasons of ministry. Singleness doesn't mean you can't go. Marriage doesn't mean you have to move out. Having children doesn't mean you're disqualified. When your children start going to school it doesn't mean you have to go back home. When your children start to date it doesn't mean you have to run away. Ministry approaches may and often should change in light of these shifts, but families can live meaningfully among the urban poor and engage their community for transformation regardless of the season of life they find themselves in.

Your Family of Origin

Your role in your family of origin will likely change as you become an incarnational leader. If you are emotionally close, your family may feel a deep sense of responsibility for you and may or may not let you go very easily. This can be true of anyone, but I have seen it especially in younger adults, single women, and individuals from highly communal cultures. Something similar may happen to those with grown children, including older adults ministering incarnationally as a second career. It is important to prayerfully consider how you can continue a relationship with your family across lifestyle differences and often a great distance. There may be some instances where God will give you peace about a broken relationship as you move toward your calling, but usually there is a way to stay on good terms after the transition.

Determining your responsibility to your parents and extended family as an incarnational leader is a highly individual process. I know a single man who took his widowed mother to live in an urban poor community with him because he felt responsible to care for her. This is a rare case, and your responsibility will probably have more to do with keeping in touch. We Skype and e-mail family in the US at least once a week, mostly to give my parents updates on our sons. The frequency of communication back home should be reasonable, and not a burden on your ministry. We cannot have a meaningful presence when we spend all our free time and most of our emotional energy online keeping up with friends and family, but there should be some contact.

Your Spouse

In the high-stress environment of an urban poor community, spouses working as a ministry team can be more sustainable and more powerful than two people acting alone. A big part of their ministry role will be praying for each other and helping each other to clearly evaluate their decisions. They will collaborate by combining their skills and temperaments, and they will roughly double the number of relationships in the community between them. Even if one spouse ministers vocationally while one retains a separate career, they can still act as a team in most of these ways.

I was blessed to meet Ema through living in her community, so continuing our life together in that context was a given as the relationship progressed. However, if you are seriously dating or married when you first move toward incarnational ministry, it is important to begin an intentional dialogue about whether you are called to become a ministry team.

Your Children

If you have children, your family may still be called to minister together. As God's call to Abraham included moving his family,[48] it seems to be more the norm rather than the exception for God to call whole families, children and all. Even though it can feel conflicting to choose to raise our children in less-than-ideal spaces, we need to be open to what God wants to do in their young lives as well.

My experience as a parent has come from raising my child in an urban poor community since birth. This was extremely difficult at first, and I can certainly understand why many couples consider moving out of an urban poor community when they start having children. When I showed my parents a photo of Zach at six months in the middle of a squatter community, I was repeatedly told, "You have to get him out of there." However, after a lot of prayer, we decided to stay. The advantage of our situation is that Zach did not go through culture or poverty shock in the urban poor community. He is perfectly at home in Botocan.

Smaller exposures to urban poverty may open up conversations with kids about relocating. A short stay in an urban poor community is built into the training model at Servant Partners, and this training is especially critical for families who have never traveled or experienced poverty together. This was the situation for the Brown family, whose children were ages seven, four, and two when they arrived in Manila. The children expressed their poverty and culture shock through misbehavior and acting out of character. The parents understood their children's stress and responded with an appropriate balance of support and behavioral expectations. Positively, the children shared that they felt they learned more about Jesus because of the poverty they saw. They also stopped complaining about things being unfair. The trip helped the children to emotionally prepare for their move to an urban poor community long term.[49]

Since Zach and then Ezra were born, we no longer live as simply as we did, as we now understand our home as a space to minister through parenting our sons and making sure they have what they need to flourish. Other new parents have had to switch homes because of safety concerns. The Hsieh family in Los Angeles moved to a ground floor unit because the stairs in their apartment were unsafe for carrying a baby up and down.[50] This is not about sacrificing our children on the altar of ministry. With flexibility, we can do what's best for our children and still live meaningfully in an urban poor community. The following are some of the parameters that parents will need to be conscious of as they raise their children in slum communities.

OPTIONS FOR EDUCATION. Education is a key concern for parents living incarnationally among the urban poor. When Zach was close to turning four years old, his education became a significant concern. In the process of looking for a preschool, we considered all of our options, from the elite preschools to the ones located within our community. Some of the elite preschools were well out of our price range and required extensive commutes each day. Others were more realistic in cost and were a reasonable commute.

The preschool we finally decided on was a Christian preschool located in our community, run by a nearby middle-class church. We decided on this preschool mainly because one of Zach's good friends in the community was also enrolled there. It is a Christian-based education within walking distance from our home. We also have the extra benefit of being able to meet the parents of other students, as one of us has to pick up Zach every day and wait outside with the other parents.

This preschool works for Zach because he is already fluent in Tagalog, the most common Filipino language used in Manila, so language is not a struggle for him. He is also half Filipino, so he does not look significantly different from the other children. If Zach stood out racially or were raised in the West, we might have had to send him to a private school so that he would not be a target for either bullying or special treatment, and because the teachers would be more familiar with multicultural education.

Low-quality academics in local schools can be overcome by taking advantage of the wide variety of specialized educational opportunities offered. During the summer, our church hosts various youth activities such as art and dance lessons. Zach has grown to love dancing through joining the youth when they dance. We also take Zach on educational trips as often as we can. The local zoo and parks allow him to see and learn about different kinds of animals. We have made the investment of time and money to have Zach take part in various educational activities available in the city. We have even planned some of our family vacations as educational ventures.

Parents should take the time to research all of their educational options, keeping in mind the child's specific needs. Some will excel in public school with lots of extracurricular involvement in the evenings or on weekends. Others will excel in a private school that provides a more specialized, well-rounded education. Still others will do best by being homeschooled. One woman who grew up on the mission field is thankful that her missionary parents took into account that each child was different and each year other factors might also be different. Her parents talked with each of the children about what they saw as their needs. In the same school year, one child might be in private school while other children might be in public school.[51] This takes a huge effort on the part of the parents, which is not always feasible. Families need to find which education solution works for them and realize they do not have to be locked into one decision.

PHYSICAL WELL-BEING. Children's safety is a major concern for many parents. Safety hazards abound in urban poor communities, and children are not often aware enough of their surroundings to avoid them. In Balic-Balic, a 6-year-old boy was killed when he was playing behind a television and his ear touched an open wire. In Botocan, a baby recently died when he fell down the stairs.

Not every community is the same, and parents need to learn which risks are present in theirs. Are there empty buildings or open fields that might be too dangerous to allow your kids to play in, even if less consistently supervised children do? Are children frequently kidnapped or molested in your community? Do violent gangs pose a risk—for stray bullets or eventual involvement?

Honestly viewing the risks, without either paranoia or inattentiveness, will better enable parents to protect their children.

It is important to give yourself flexibility to break away from the norms of your community in raising your children. When the Brown family arrived in South Asia, they quickly decided that though the train is the major form of transportation in their city, it does not work for their family. Because it is so crowded, traveling with three young children is dangerous. They decided to go with different transportation options rather than risk having their children trampled or separated from them in the dense crowds.[52]

Realistically, we are quite safe in Botocan. There are many people out all the time, and the community has a twenty-four-hour security force that patrols the alleyways. We have also built enough positive relationships so that people look out for us. After dark one evening, Zach went missing. A three-year-old lost in the middle of a slum at night: any parent would be horrified. But without panicking, I went down all the main walkways, checking to see if anyone had seen him. Several of the neighborhood children helped in the search. We eventually found him with one of his older friends. He was safe the whole time. If this happened in a wealthy community, he could have been in significantly more danger because of the risk of being hit by a car.

When Zach is older, his physical safety at school will become more of a factor. As a parent, I am responsible for the safety of my child. Therefore, I want to be fairly sure that his school will not allow him to get excessively beat up or killed by his rougher classmates.

When it comes to health risks, some incarnational leaders can be overprotective, while others may put their children in unnecessary danger. Some risks, such as the risk of developing asthma from urban smog, are built in and must be counted as costs from the outset. Others can be avoided by teaching hand-washing and avoiding contact with the sick, even if these are not culturally common precautions. In addition, incarnational leaders can use their knowledge of health and nutrition for the benefit of their own children and for the community.

Life is not about being safe; it is about being obedient to God. My prayer for Zach and Ezra, as well as for myself, is that God would keep us alive as long as we can still contribute to the Kingdom. Incarnational leaders have experienced the deep pain of having their babies die. Other parents had their teenage children come home covered in blood from being beat up. Recognizing that these are real and heart-wrenching traumas, the place where God has called your family to be is still absolutely the best place for your children to grow up. If we want the best for our children, we need to continually choose to be in the center of God's will.

BAD INFLUENCES. Helping Zach to understand the bad influences and sins he sees is another major struggle for us. During an outdoor Vacation Bible School with neighborhood children, I noticed two very young children who were about five. They put dirt in a clear plastic bag and were flicking the bag with the dirt in it. I finally asked the children what they were doing, and without hesitation they replied, "We're playing drug dealer."

We have given up trying to shelter Zach from the sins in our community. At age three, he put a chopstick in his mouth and told me, "Look dad, I have a cigarette." Later that same day, he was playing with his friends and they were pretending to be eating. They were offering each other different kinds of food when his friend asked him if he wanted any liquor. "Yes," Zach responded, and he began offering imaginary liquor to his other friends.

While some of our neighbors think it is funny when young kids use extremely bad language, we have tried to teach Zach that there are certain words and fingers he should not use. Before Zach turned three, he knew more bad words in Tagalog than I did. In fact, most of the bad words I know in Tagalog I learned from him.

There are bad influences in every community. As a general rule of thumb, we should not assume wealthy children are better influences than poor children. By the time middle-class suburban kids are in middle school, they will not only be exposed to sex and drugs, but also be pressured to try them. I know a drug addict who first used drugs in the parking lot of a suburban church after youth group. Kids are going to learn about violence, drunkenness, drugs, sex, and bad words no matter how sheltered they are. Zach is just learning them a few years earlier than his middle-class peers. Soon, little Ezra will too. We may not like it and we do our best to curb it, but we have come to terms with it as parents. We recognize that our children's moral character, like the moral character of the poor, is much deeper and richer than the crudeness we might perceive on the surfaces of their behavior.

EMOTIONAL TRAUMA. Children are even more likely than adults to develop anxiety problems associated with witnessing suffering and the fear of violence. The older the children are when they enter the urban poor environment, the harder time they will have adjusting to it. Parents need to be aware of their children's experiences and react with empathy to negative behaviors that result from emotional trauma. An incarnational leader in the Southern

Philippines tells the painful struggle of his daughter's anxiety over kidnapping fears.

> To be honest, we didn't really think there was a high risk of us being kidnapped or killed in the Southern Philippines. Admittedly, there were a few missionaries who have been kidnapped over the years. I had been personally threatened to be shot if I went outside our house in Manila. So we knew there were risks and that in itself was a little stressful, but not overwhelmingly so.
>
> After two years in the Southern Philippines, our seven-year-old daughter, Tirzah, became increasingly anxious. There were fifty kidnappings in our city of 200,000 in the last year we lived there. Sometimes we'd hear gunfire or a grenade exploding. One morning, we were all at home when we heard gunshots. Our neighbor came in to warn us a kidnapping was in progress.
>
> Occasionally, our neighbors and friends would talk about kidnappings with children present. One day, our landlord told Tirzah that he hoped her mother and father wouldn't be kidnapped. As a seven-year-old, she was unable to process this idea and began having nightmares about being left alone with no one to look after her. Over time, her anxiety generalized into a fear of being alone at any time. Even though we only lived in a two-room house, Tirzah wouldn't even go to the bathroom by herself, and when we went out she would hang on to us fearfully.
>
> Tirzah had nightmares every night, sometimes more than once a night. Often, she would appear to be semi-awake, muttering and looking all around her. At the

time, we didn't understand she was experiencing night terrors—a common phenomenon with young children. All we could do was comfort her, be present with her, and pray for her. We helped her to learn to pray in the midst of those nightmare-experiences.

We tried to find counseling to process the issues but were unable to find this kind of help in the Southern Philippines. We hoped for recovery for a long time, but as our daughter's anxiety worsened, we became increasingly concerned. My wife was struggling emotionally and felt she wasn't accomplishing much. At the time, I was only able to work at about fifty percent capacity, which wasn't worth the stress our family was experiencing. I still enjoyed my involvement in the community and local churches, but I recognized the cost was too high for such little output. I decided to spend a day at a quiet Catholic grotto in prayer and fasting to seek God's will. Sometime during that afternoon, I experienced a sense of peace about leaving the Philippines, and I concluded this was the Lord's guidance.

Since that time I've never doubted the decision to leave. Back in Australia, we took our daughter to a Christian psychiatrist who diagnosed her with separation anxiety disorder. He was able to help her express her fears in story form and acknowledge we were all safe now. After a few months, her anxiety symptoms began to diminish—to the point where they were no longer a major concern. However, the nightmares continued for years afterwards, gradually diminishing in frequency with each month that passed. Tirzah is now in her fifth year of university, studying a double degree in law and creative writing. She is actively involved in a young adult group at church and leads a fulfilling life.

Tirzah added the following reflections:

The fear of losing people did transfer onto other things later. For example, once (I might have been ten), I was told a scary story that made me afraid we would all be murdered while we slept. This caused anxiety getting to sleep and I woke frequently during the night. This probably lasted a couple of years with decreasing severity, until I finished high school.[53]

Incarnational leaders need to be sensitive about how their children are really coping and provide the help needed for their children. In some cases, the family may need to move out of their urban poor community or leave the particular cross-cultural ministry setting altogether. In other cases, professional help and lifestyle adjustments can help the child recover a much-needed sense of security and well-being while still in the field. Your child's emotional health needs to be prayerfully observed and considered in conversation with your spouse.

GOING "BACK HOME"? When Zach was three years old, we had to help him process culture shock when we took him to the United States to visit his grandparents. Being exposed to different kinds of food was his main struggle. Traveling made it difficult to have control over our food. Zach struggled at his first burger joint in the United States. Restaurants in Manila that sell burgers also sell spaghetti. He tried to order spaghetti, but of course they did not carry spaghetti. Zach was too young to understand, so that was hard for him. Some of the wealth was also beyond his comprehension. On various occasions, he referred to people's sheds as houses. Why not? Sheds look very close to squatter homes in both style and size.

We had an embarrassing moment when he urinated in a neighbor's front yard in front of several people. A few days later, at a public pool, Zach climbed out of the pool and urinated on the grass. His five-year-old cousin was amazed at what he did and kept telling everyone about it. Another adult asked if we punished Zach, and I explained that I did not because he was not from the United States. Male urination in public is the norm in urban poor areas in Manila, and it is unfair to punish a child for behavior that is accepted in one place but not another. Zach's grandmother did, however, try to explain to him that while in the United States he should try to use the toilet.

When Zach gets older, we will probably need to help him process more complicated questions about his relationship to American culture. Relating to his grandparents and extended family may be difficult, and I hope that he will feel comfortable asking me for help and advice as he learns more about his background and relatives.

PARENTING JOYS. Church planter and community developer Michael Duncan shares his journey of relocating to Manila with young children in his book, *Costly Mission*.[54] While he emphasizes that following Christ as a family is more important than avoiding the suffering of our children, I want to encourage families to realize that they can in fact thrive in urban poor environments. Families need to know that it is okay to prepare for and accommodate the well-being of their children by finding educational options and parameters of safety that work for their kids. While there is no denying the struggles associated with raising a child in an urban poor community, there are also many benefits. Urban poor communities can be wonderful places to grow up, and to be a parent.

Parents raising children in an urban poor environment are more in tune with the truth that our kids don't really belong to us—they belong to God. There are many aspects of the urban poor environment we cannot control, so we have to trust God or we will become overburdened by stress. However, we also have the privilege of helping children successfully navigate a walk with God in a vibrant environment.

Building strong bonds with your children is one of the best ways to help overcome any negatives and embrace the positive aspects of urban poor family life. As a family, we have decided not to have the boys in daycare or hire a regular babysitter, not because it is wrong to do so, but because it works quite well for us to keep them with us. They go almost everywhere with at least one of their parents, from errands to church meetings to social occasions. We often go on trips to local parks and playgrounds. Every Saturday that it does not rain, we go with the youth to the University of the Philippines. The boys always come along. I am hoping the investment we are putting into bonding with them as young children will pay off when they are teenagers faced with more temptations than I can imagine.

A businessman friend shared with me that he believes Zach will benefit from his experience of growing up in a squatter community, and this was largely because of the amazing empathy that the toddler already displayed. By the time he was three years old, Zach was aware of the poverty around him. The opportunity to give comes up so often that Zach instinctively knows we should give food to the hungry and drink to the thirsty. One day, we were visiting in an area that had many homeless families. Zach immediately said that we should give food and jewelry to them. When

I pointed out that I do not even have jewelry, Zach insisted that since they do not have anything we should help them with more than food. I was amazed that my three-year-old had come up with this insight. There is no need for a Ph.D. in development to know it takes more than a bowl of rice to end poverty.

Finally, we hope that Zach and Ezra will develop both faith in God and confidence in their own social skills through their experience in the communities. They will know how to handle a lot, both emotionally and practically. They will understand multiple languages, cultures, and ways of living. And they will know that we are sustained by God even in the midst of chaos.

Conclusion

Our families are fundamentally affected by our transition into full-time ministry. As your roles change, you will need to comfort and assure your family of origin, prayerfully make decisions with your spouse and ministry partner, and carefully navigate a new set of parenting challenges. Parents have to be careful that their children are not physically or emotionally damaged by their environment, but they also should not be so overprotective that they miss the many benefits of parenting a child in an urban poor community.

[48] Gen. 12:5
[49] Interview with the "Browns," August 9, 2011. Indian Wells, CA.
[50] Interview with Tom Hsieh, August 5, 2011. Indian Wells, CA.
[51] Interview with Betty Sue Brewster, August 8, 2011. Indian Wells, CA.
[52] Interview with the "Browns."
[53] E-mail interview with Ashley Withers, August 4, 2011.
[54] Michael Duncan, *Costly Mission: Following Christ into the Slums* (Monrovia, CA: MARC, 1996).

PART TWO:

PRACTICING SUSTAINABILITY IN YOUR INCARNATIONAL MINISTRY

8

SELF-APPRAISAL

IN ORDER TO DISCERN and sustain a calling in Christ, it is crucial that we have a realistic appraisal of ourselves—our calling, our gifts, and our limitations. An incarnational leader among the urban poor (or in any other context) must know his or her own spiritual, mental, and physical makeup, as well as those of any family and team members who minister with them. This is crucial for discerning both whether one is called into incarnational ministry, and what type of ministry one should develop.

If you are already established as an urban poor minister, it is by no means too late to self-reflect. In fact, being aware of your own internal conditions and motivations is a key responsibility that you will carry throughout your ministry.

Are You Called to the Urban Poor?

Incarnational ministry among the urban poor is not for everyone. In fact, *it is not even for everyone who has a heart for the urban poor.* There are certainly other ways to influence society to be more welcoming to the poor, a few of which will be discussed below.

Ultimately, the only reason for becoming an incarnational leader in this context is that God is calling and equipping you to do so.

Calling is a vital component of sustainability. Eighty-seven percent of incarnational leaders surveyed mentioned calling as key to long-term sustainability among the urban poor.[55] For some, God's call is very specific, sometimes to an exact location or a specific time commitment. For others, it is a more general sense of being an ally to the poor, and there is more creative flexibility and freedom in the application.

God's call can come through conversations with wise counselors, situational confirmations, the Bible, and prayer. It is wise to wait on God so that we do not jump into things before we are ready. At the same time, we should not be stuck waiting for God's calling in our lives. I have worked with several young adults who practically put their lives on hold while they waited for a clear calling from God. Sometimes we can only see God's calling for us by exploring around the edges of it.

Pause and Reflect:

1. After reading through Section I, what aspects of urban poor ministry resonate with or attract you? What aspects seem most difficult?
2. As of now, what sense do you have of God's calling? When you imagine your journey with Christ over the next 10 years, how does urban poverty come into play?
3. What events and circumstances are key to your discernment story so far? (See *My Story* in the introduction for one example of a discernment story.)

For Those Who Are Called Elsewhere

Incarnational ministry is certainly not limited to ministers moving into poor communities, even though that is the popular association. Building meaningful relationships and engagement for transformation is relevant for people of all social classes. I hope that if you have determined that urban poverty is not your context, you would continue to make creative applications from this text, as well as to support others who walk with the poor.

If you are a pastor among the middle and upper class, living in their neighborhood may be much less vital. This is because wealthier communities are often centered at work, school, or social spaces, rather than in the members' homes. Neighbors in wealthy housing areas may not even know each other. The mobility of the wealthy can be an asset, opening up opportunities for ministry outside of the immediate area of the church. Middle-class, lower-middle-class, and cross-class congregations may have diverse readings on these issues, and it is still extremely important to make sure your programming is relevant to members who are affected by justice issues in their neighborhoods, as well as inclusive of those for whom traveling is a hardship.

I have a pastor friend who is involved in a big bike organization whose members all own high-powered motorcycles. This is an expensive hobby, but the pastor has been able to have a powerful ministry by becoming one of the group. When he first joined, most of the members were either neutral or hostile toward Christianity. However, after this pastor's involvement in this organization, many of them have begun to look favorably upon Christians. He is now even called upon to pray for their trips before they begin a ride.

Specialized ministries among students, veterans, battered women, or other groups should be as incarnational as possible. While it is not usually feasible to literally become a student in order to be better at student ministry, for example, it is important to be present on campus for more than just programming so that you can understand the issues affecting students. Being present by living reasonably close can help you to open your home as a ministry space and invite the community more fully into your life. Engagement toward the Kingdom is also crucial. Striving for justice across class, race, and gender is often a central concern on campuses, in social spaces, and in various industries. Helping others to discern a call to urban poor or other ministries can be a vital role within the Kingdom as well.

None of these suggestions are meant to distract those who are called to work among the poor. However, I want to acknowledge and affirm that Christians are called to every sector of society. If you are called elsewhere, use discretion and creativity to apply these lessons on incarnational ministry among the urban poor, and keep in mind that your discernment process may lead you closer to the poor over time.

Pause and Reflect:

1. Have you experienced a call to a specific community or group where you might minister?
2. What aspects of urban poor ministry seem to be most relevant to your current context?
3. How can you be an ally to the poor while ministering among those who are not poor?

What Makes a Long-Term Leader?

In many ways, sustainability in incarnational ministry among the urban poor comes down to the person. All incarnational leaders will face traumas, failures, and suffering. Some will stay, while others will move on. Since the attitude of the person plays a factor in sustainability, it is helpful to examine some of the characteristics of those who last and those who don't.

The purpose of the following lists is for self-reflection. We need to honestly examine ourselves in order to truly assess how our attitudes affect the sustainability of our incarnational ministry. If you have many of the qualities in the first list, it does not mean that you are called to urban poverty. If you have many of the qualities in the second, it does not mean that you are not called—but it probably means that you have some things to work on before you begin ministering.

An incarnational leader is likely to last long term if he/she:

- [ ] Loves God, the urban poor, and his/her city
- [ ] Has a strong conviction concerning God's call
- [ ] Handles criticism, rejection, and failure well
- [ ] Is able to live flexibly, with compromise
- [ ] Has a persistent sense of humor
- [ ] Prioritizes relationships
- [ ] Has a never-quit attitude
- [ ] Thinks and acts collaboratively, in community
- [ ] Regularly practices life-giving spiritual disciplines
- [ ] Is willing to learn
- [ ] Has a hopeful outlook
- [ ] Stays open to personal development
- [ ] Accepts that he/she cannot change everything
- [ ] Practices healthy patterns of work and rest

An incarnational leader is unlikely to last long term if he/she:

- ☐ Focuses on how much he/she sacrificed
- ☐ Ministers as a protest against something
- ☐ Ministers only to fulfill needs, not to build relationships
- ☐ Promotes a personal agenda
- ☐ Has an attitude of entitlement
- ☐ Believes the poor are inferior
- ☐ Needs to be the hero
- ☐ Focuses on material/external experiences
- ☐ Complains constantly
- ☐ Loses temper easily
- ☐ Panics in chaos and conflict
- ☐ Has grand plans to end poverty
- ☐ Is private or self-protective
- ☐ Is spiritually stagnant or immature
- ☐ Is easily discouraged

Those who live among the poor by choice are not somehow better than the urban poor themselves or those who choose to live elsewhere. Incarnational leaders need to avoid the temptation to become self-righteous or to believe that we cannot and do not fall into the latter category—we quite often do!

If you see any of the latter qualities consistently in your own life, bring that concern to God and to advisors you trust. You may want to set some time aside, before or during your ministry, to intentionally reflect on your thought patterns and prayerfully lean toward better ones.

Pause and Reflect:

1. Go through the lists and check off the qualities that you see in yourself. Be honest with yourself, and ask for input from others.
2. Without condemning yourself, which list represents your current temperament and spiritual state better?
3. What sustainable qualities do you need to practice and pray for? What unsustainable qualities do you need God to help you move away from?

What Are Your Limitations?

Because the lifestyle of the urban poor minister can be intense and demanding, it is easy to doubt your own ability to meet the challenge. Realism and humility are important. However, God is in the habit of calling unlikely people to ministry. If fear and self-doubt are keeping you from pursuing a call that you know you hear, be encouraged. God will walk with you to overcome or even use your limitations.

My friends Lisa and Eric are incarnational leaders in South Los Angeles. From the start of their marriage, they planned to live in the inner city for life. They eventually decided to move to Los Angeles under a two-year domestic internship with Servant Partners, but about six months into their internship, Lisa suddenly became urgently sick. First, her hand went numb, and within twelve hours, she was in the hospital on a ventilator. She became paralyzed from the neck down.

Lisa and Eric wanted to continue living in their neighborhood, but at first this seemed impossible. Lisa was told she would be a target for robbery. There were lots of internal questions as to how effective they would be in the ministry. They wondered how Lisa would be able to meet neighbors and live meaningfully in the community. Trusting that God would eventually make a way, they made the difficult decision to stay. They decided that their best option would be to buy a home, because if they rented it would be very difficult to make the home wheelchair accessible. God opened the doors for them to buy a house and make the necessary modifications for a wheelchair.

It turned out meeting neighbors came about quite naturally for Lisa. Neighbors began to come over and hang out with her on their porch, and relationships started to form. She has found that having a physical disability helps neighbors to have a way to give back to her. Neighbors feel at home in their house because they go over to help Lisa. She reflects, "It changes our status a little bit and makes us more approachable."[56]

In the Kingdom, our perceived limitation can actually be an advantage. Lisa's handicap led to others being comfortable to freely express their thoughts and emotions to her, paving the way for deep and meaningful relationships. Being in a wheelchair has even enabled Lisa to minister to her neighbors with disabilities. Lisa and Eric are able to share their wheelchair-accessible van with others in the neighborhood. As Lisa has gotten better, she is able to go out with neighbors, which gives her more freedom in her ministry. Far from preventing her from being an incarnational leader in an urban poor community, Lisa's disability has enabled them to live meaningfully in their community and engage their community for transformation.

Physical disabilities, severe allergies, different personalities or minds—all of these can be part of your presence in an urban poor community. However, it is important that you are aware of your limitations and your unique needs and accommodate them. This is the only way to do ministry long term.

Pause and Reflect:

1. What limitations do you feel may come into play in your ministry?
2. What do you need to do to accommodate those limitations so that you can sustain your ministry long term?
3. How might God use those limitations for the Kingdom?

Who Should Discern With You?

Becoming an incarnational leader is not about being a lone hero. Many others will be affected by your decision—some more directly than others. If you are married, I can almost guarantee that God will not call you into urban ministry without also calling your spouse. Those who have a spouse and/or dependents, as well as adults who are dependent on others due to disability or other factors, need to treat discernment as a team activity from the outset. However, everyone should involve spiritual advisors and their closest friends and family members fairly early on.

If you are a parent, your children's ages and maturity levels will help you determine if and when to involve them in the process of choosing to relocate. There is a real extent to which we must make decisions on behalf of our children. A child who has never experienced life in an urban poor community might not know how to thoughtfully consider whether they even want to relocate. However, it is important to make this decision with love and empathy toward your child's experience. Any conversations with children beforehand need to deal frankly with the sense of loss that they may experience as they deal with urban stress and live with fewer material things. But they should also emphasize the many opportunities to make friends and help others, both of which are very attractive ideas to many children.

In the previous chapter, we discussed the ways your family of origin might be affected by relocation at greater length. After reviewing that chapter, take a moment to consider your own loved ones.

Pause and Reflect:

1. Who would necessarily relocate with you (spouse, dependents)? How do you envision (or remember) your first conversations with these people?
2. Who else will be directly affected by your relocation (close family members/friends, significant others, your children's grandparents)? What can you realistically promise about keeping in touch and visiting as you begin the conversation?
3. Whose additional support would you value throughout your process (mentors, parents, pastors)?

What Will You Need When You're Leading?

Once you have determined that you are going to lean into a call to urban poor ministry, self-appraisal will help you to choose ministry parameters that allow for both effectiveness and sustainability. This is not about worshipping comfort or seeking an easy way to proclaim Jesus among the urban poor. It is about realistically taking into account how God made each of us and our families, and settling in for a long haul.

My first attempt at incarnational ministry led to burnout within a year. At that time, I was living with several youth at the same level of poverty as those around me. This meant there were always people in my one-room house. When I left for class, someone would be home; after a long day, I would return to a packed house. As an introvert, I lacked the personal time I needed. These days, Ema and I choose to close the door on occasion so that we have some much-needed time to recharge our social batteries.

Your physical needs should also be honored. In general it is advisable to have access to a decent bathroom and to have some control over your food and water. A bad bathroom situation can result in health problems and become a major point of stress. Every squatter home I have lived in had its own bathroom, even if it did not have running water. There are some urban poor communities that do not have bathrooms. In these communities, incarnational leaders will need to learn how to stay healthy. There are ways to get around not having a bathroom, but it will be a challenge.

Now that we have two young sons, Ema and I must consider their needs as well as our own. They need a safe place to play and learn. We have tried to make our home such a place, which has meant maximizing floor space where they can play, as well as investing in toys, books, and educational games for them and their friends. Children's books are not common in Botocan, so we keep them out for other children to use. This has been helpful for Zach and Ezra's socialization, as well as for us to be able to keep the young children in the neighborhood interested in learning.

Your specific ministry role is a significant factor when it comes to determining how you will actually live in the community. My current ministry roles include teaching in a local seminary and training with Servant Partners. This means that I need control over my time in order to prepare. Ema was a counseling student when we first moved into Botocan, so she also needed protected control over her time to study. This makes it especially important that we have our own space, rather than living with another family or in community.

We moved into Botocan with the specific purpose of planting a church, so our home had to be something that could meet both our personal and ministry needs. God provided the perfect place for us. We are very close to the main basketball court in Botocan where most community events are held, and our location is both known and accessible to the entire community.

Pause and Reflect:

1. What physical and mental health issues do you need to accommodate for a safe and fruitful ministry?
2. How much control over food do you need? Do you have allergies or dietary restrictions?
3. How much control over time do you need? Are you sensitive to sleep deprivation? How much alone time do you require to be functional? Optimal?

Conclusion

A sustainable ministry must be rooted in reality. Minister must be able to realistically evaluate whether they are called to live among the urban poor, and what accommodations they might need to build a life there. This means understanding and honoring the unique gifts and limits of the ministering leader and his/her family.

---

[55] See Appendix B.
[56] Interview with Lisa Barlow, July 6, 2011. Los Angeles, CA.

9

PREPARATION AND EXPOSURE

FAITH IN YOUR CALL does not mean that you have to or should jump into it blind. Taking your potential role seriously means learning and experiencing as much as you can about ministering in urban poverty contexts as you explore your options.

Growing Spiritually

The best preparation for incarnational ministry among the urban poor is focusing on developing one's relationship with Jesus. Sixty-one percent of incarnational leaders stated that focusing more on spiritual disciplines would have better prepared them for life among the urban poor.[57] In other words, it is more important to develop healthy spiritual disciplines and inner character than specific ministry skills, which can be picked up along the way. We need to be emotionally stable, have spiritual roots that go deep, and constantly drink from the living water of Jesus. Incarnational leaders should strive to be able to say along with Paul, "Be imitators of me, as I am of Christ."[58]

Incarnational ministry is an inner journey in Christ as much as an outer journey in the community. We are transformed through the process of living meaningfully among the urban poor and engaging the community for transformation. We will be transformed by pain, by failure, and by joy. Spiritual growth should help prepare us to transform toward the image of Christ, rather than away from it.

Consistent spiritual disciplines are a key way to give God space to do this work in you. If you are not familiar with spiritual disciplines, take a peek ahead at Chapter 14, where some sustaining spiritual disciplines are suggested. It is also important to grow together with a mentor, peer accountability partner/group, or both.

Pause and Reflect:

1. How would you describe your spiritual walk this week? How would you like to be able to describe it?
2. In what spiritual disciplines or other activities has God historically been present with you? How can you further embrace these activities?
3. Who helps you to grow spiritually? How might they participate in your preparation?

Getting to Know Your Current Neighbors

Many of us are simply not experienced in neighborliness. Westerners in particular tend to know relatively little about the people in their communities. Instantly switching from no contact to constant contact is an unrealistic expectation; it is best to start building your capacity for relationships with those around you now. This does not necessarily mean developing deep attachments, especially if it is likely that you will soon relocate. However, it might mean learning a few names, hosting a meal or two, and maybe praying together.

If you plan to minister among the urban poor, it is important that you are not shielding yourself from your current poor neighbors. No matter where you are in the world, poverty is not far from you. There may be certain neighborhoods near you that are looked down on; there may be opportunities to engage with homeless men, women, and kids. Seeking out ways of serving and relating to these neighbors will present countless opportunities to learn from their wisdom and experience, as well as their struggles and unique perspectives.

Stretching your role in your current community to be more like the role you sense you are called into among the poor is a wonderful way to feel out your call, curb transitional stress, and make friends who can support you.

Pause and Reflect:

1. What do you love about your current community?
2. How would you describe your current interactions in your neighborhood?
3. What can you do to connect with your neighbors, especially your poor neighbors, more intentionally and consistently?

Education and Training

The word *education* has many meanings, and I want to emphasize that there is no special degree or credential required to live and work among the urban poor. However, if we're passionate about being neighbors to the poor, we should be aware of all of the resources that could help to make us better at it. If you do enjoy the academic route, several seminaries across the globe offer Masters Degrees in Transformational Urban Leadership (MATUL), which focus on ministry in urban poor communities. But no matter where you are, there may be classes, workshops, or trainings available to you that focus on ministry, community organizing, urban poverty, or related topics. If your ministry could benefit from specific skills, such as first aid, cooking, preaching, Bible study, or mastery of a new language, keep your eyes open for opportunities to learn through both classes and hands-on experiences. There may be organizations in your area that offer free valuable training to volunteers and interns in any number of areas.

Your own personal reading list can be an amazing tool for ministry preparation. In my own journey, Viv Grigg's *Companion to the Poor* was an essential turning point in both discernment and preparation. At the back of this book, you will find a bibliography which contains this and dozens of other valuable titles. My recommendations for next reads are indicated in bold.

A note as you seek out education is that we need to prioritize what the poor say about themselves as we study poverty. While it is sometimes necessary to look at statistics and trends which the poor themselves might not meaningfully experience, any education that does not hold the human experience of the poor at the center is incomplete. As we enter into these communities, we must be humble about the severe limits of our academic education and maintain a learning posture toward our neighbors.

Pause and Reflect:

1. What has your education on urban poverty looked like so far? (Academic? Experiential?)
2. What topics would you like to learn about? What skills would you like to master?
3. What other books are on your reading list?

Exposure Trips and Internships

Short-term exposure trips are a great way to get a glimpse of global urban poverty and to begin seeing how God is at work among the urban poor. Many sending organizations offer international internships where teams get exposure to life in a squatter community as they receive practical training in urban poor ministry. Daniel spent three months with us in Botocan as a short-term intern with Servant Partners. He expressed how the experience of living in a squatter community helped him to learn the benefits of incarnational ministry and was significant in clarifying his call.[59] He came into the internship with the perspective that he was there to seek God. Living in the community and challenging himself to interact with neighbors helped him to have a posture of learning and to be receptive to what God had for him.

By their very nature, short-term exposure trips are not incarnational. There is minimal personal investment and there are no roots in the community. In reality, short-term trips are more about God transforming those who go rather than transforming the community to which they are sent. However, because of the harm and confusion that the pop-in/pop-out ministry model can cause in the community, I would still prioritize being hosted by permanent incarnational teams during your temporary stay. This also allows you to learn from committed incarnational leaders.[60]

One of the most valuable aspects of exposure trips are that they help to induce and process poverty shock before you begin ministering. Many people in the West were sheltered from extreme poverty growing up, and very few have had meaningful experiences in the midst of it. Just like being immersed in an unfamiliar culture, suddenly being immersed in a different economic class can cause disorientation and stress. You may be unsure of how to respond in social situations, you may feel like you do not belong, and you may be overwhelmed with discomfort as your norms begin to shift. With extreme poverty, there is also an added layer of emotional difficulty as you come to see that real people—with names and personalities and human value—live in conditions that you may have before thought were unimaginable.

Just as with culture shock, poverty shock comes in waves and may be especially strong in the first few months. It is a good idea to ground yourself by finding settings that are more like your experience at home, as well as eating familiar foods and doing familiar activities. This could mean staying overnight away from the urban poor community every so often. Some groups in Manila stay outside the community once a week; for others is it less often. It is important to give yourself the freedom to get away when you need to. You can see how an internship or short-term trip might be a better environment to process a new awareness of poverty.

If you do not prepare yourself for, and properly respond to, poverty shock, burnout is a serious risk. It can also lead to making misguided decisions or coming to resent the poor. This does not mean we should normalize poverty to the point that oppression and exploitation of the poor becomes accepted as the way things are. Engagement for transformation, whether through a Bible study or community organizing or other means, must be carried out with a mindset of eventually addressing the larger issues of poverty and injustice.

Pause and Reflect:

1. To what extent have you experienced or witnessed poverty in your life so far? Have you already experienced poverty shock?
2. What experience has led most directly to your interest in working with the poor?
3. What is your next step toward better understanding and feeling at home among the urban poor?

Conclusion

Once you have chosen to live among the urban poor, you can begin to adopt a mindset of growing toward a ministerial role. You should do this by grounding your own faith, becoming a better neighbor in your current setting, and seeking experiences which will immersively educate you about the life experiences of the urban poor and the realities of living alongside them.

---

[57] See Appendix B
[58] 1 Cor. 11:1
[59] Interview with Daniel Groot, August 10, 2011. Indian Hills, CA.
[60] See Appendix C for a list of incarnational organizations. Opportunities for internships and exposure trips are often available through them.

10

CHOOSING ANCHOR INSTITUTIONS

IN ORDER TO RELOCATE to a new place, it is necessary to get established in that place in some way. If you simply wander into a community and announce that you are the new neighbor, nobody will know what to make of you. You need a role in the community that residents understand and can relate to. This will help minimize some of the reasonable suspicions that residents might have about your sudden appearance.

Membership in multiple institutions, such as school, work, church, or missional organizations, will effectively lend structure to your life and ministry and provide natural connections to both the community and fellow leaders. Ideally, your anchoring institutions will also provide support toward your specific goal of holistic community engagement for transformation in Christ. Wisely choosing institutions is an important part of developing a ministry that will last.

School or Workplace

Since slum communities are often close to urban centers, there are many opportunities to live among the urban poor while pursuing a traditional education or career nearby. I first came to access a relationship with the urban poor in Balic-Balic while studying at Asian Theological Seminary. The school provided structure, connections to my student peers, mentors to pray for and advise me, and a legitimate base and explanation for being in the community—both on my visa and in the minds of my new neighbors.

In many cultures, being an employee or a student carries a legitimacy that might not come with being a minister. After returning to Balic-Balic with Servant Partners, I was essentially a full-time church worker for four years. The community residents did not consider the normal ministries of a church worker, such as visitation, leading Bible studies, and overseeing church programs, as work. Ema would often be asked why I did not have a job. Ever since I took a part-time volunteer teaching position at ATS, no one has commented that I need to find a job. Residents are familiar with teaching as a profession; it is a role that my neighbors can relate to. This has helped them to accept my presence in the community, and it has helped me to more clearly model to the youth that they need to seek legitimate, legal employment as well.

Initially, the role of student or language learner might be enough to legitimize a leader's presence. However, it is not a long-term role. An incarnational leader will eventually graduate or get a decent grasp on the language and be expected to move on. However, some incarnational leaders have been able to use community projects that they initiated as students to serve as their more permanent role, so this is not a bad way to start by any means.

If a full-time job in the city is the one structuring element for your presence, you may be thoroughly limited in your contact with neighbors and your leadership in the urban poor church. While you can still be a great neighbor as a full-time employee, a part-time job may give you more control over your time. It is also difficult for even a Christian employer or school to meaningfully support a ministry that you conduct outside of work or study hours, so a second anchor institution will usually be necessary. However, moving to an urban poor community while you work or study may allow you to test the waters while seeking out opportunities with these more permanent institutions.

Pause and Reflect:

1. Do you plan to work or attend classes while you minister incarnationally?
2. What qualities would you prioritize in a school or place of work?
3. Will language learning be part of your first year? How can you harness this to connect with neighbors?

Partner Church or Ministering Community

Incarnational ministry is best carried out in a ministering community. A ministry team or community of faith allows for greater flexibility regarding approaches to incarnational ministry. It allows us to encourage one another and help each other stand firm in the faith. When I am struggling, others can carry me along. When I am strong, I can carry others who are struggling. Community is an important key to the sustainability of the incarnational leader.

I entered Balic-Balic through the ministries of an existing church. The pastor who introduced me to the community hosted me during long weekends, introduced me to community members, helped me navigate local customs, and increasingly gave me leadership opportunities. It was my partnership with the church leadership that allowed me to take over his ministry and then his home the following year. Since I had been praying to actually move into Balic-Balic instead of living on campus, this was a key point where the church, and the community, genuinely took me in.

Not every community has a local church, and filling this gap might be a key part of a minister's call. However, partnering with a nearby church to accomplish this is still key. It provides many of the same opportunities as working directly under a church. The church planting team in Botocan included our family, local leaders, and members and administrators from Xaris-Faith Bible Church (XBC), a nearby cross-class church.

For those with a ministerial role that requires them to oversee multiple sites, it is important to partner with a local church or organization that has developed a meaningful presence at each site. If you belong to a denomination which sends out church planters, they may be able to provide spiritual mentorship and other key benefits of working under a church. However, I still recommend at least casually associating with local churches that are already established in the area, even if they are not from the same denomination.

Pause and Reflect:

1. What types of ministry communities have you been a part of in the past?
2. What role do you generally take on ministry or project teams? What role do you have in your current church?
3. Does your current church have any denominational links or partnerships to urban poor churches? If so, have you considered these as potential ministry sites?

Sending Organization

In my experience, it is crucial to seek out an external organization which trains, equips, and supports incarnational leaders for work and life among the urban poor. A sending organization ideally provides accountability, emotional and logistical support, and the connection to a larger movement of ministers. An organization can also connect you to resources that would be inaccessible to an individual working without an organization.

As mentioned above, some denominations have a missions and/or church planting branch built into their structure. If your passion is to live incarnationally among the urban poor, you will need to consider whether your church's sending branch is an avenue for incarnational ministry, rather than a means of simply expanding the denomination. If your church operates on one-year assignments or assumes that you will live in the suburbs and commute to your church, it may not be the best option to support you as you develop an incarnational ministry.

I recommend finding the right organization for your prayerfully developed ministry values and goals, as well as your specific circumstances and needs. The list of organizations appended in this book should help you to get started.[61] Important aspects to seek out are a broad focus (rather than a focus that is conversion or agenda driven), flexibility for the minister, training and accountability, and meaningful support networks. An organization is incarnational if it emphasizes meaningful presence through relationships and engagement for transformation. There has to be a value for being with the people, expressed by prioritizing housing and lifestyle decisions which help the minister become a neighbor to the poor. Servant Partners' model of facilitating self-raised financial support is also one that I enjoy, as my donors are my personal friends and colleagues, and I know they are committed to supporting me through the long haul—and that they are also praying for me. Other models that keep the flow of money human and holy could work just as well.

Whether through a church or a sending organization, a mentorship or apprentice relationship with a more experienced incarnational leader can be an important factor in helping new leaders flourish in their life and ministry. In this type of extended on-the-job training, new incarnational leaders are provided with emotional and prayer support to help them to process their experience of living among the urban poor. New incarnational leaders are on a steep learning curve about themselves, the urban poor, and God. Mentorships can provide a structured means of reflection as well as practical advice for facing the difficulties of this lifestyle.

Pause and Reflect:

1. What sending organizations have you encountered so far? What was your experience with them?
2. What are your priorities in choosing an organization? (Control over location, preferred funding model, level of guidance?)
3. What is your next step toward establishing or maximizing a relationship with a potential sending organization?

Conclusion

The incarnational leader needs a framework for settling into the community. This can be achieved by any combination of school/work, church association, and membership in a sending organization. Ideally, it will include all three to maximize support and efficacy in the community. When choosing your specific anchors, it is important to look for institutions that will support and make space for your community engagement toward transformation in Christ. Sustainability starts with how we establish ourselves in our locations and ministries.

[61] See Appendix C.

11

CHOOSING A MINISTRY APPROACH

THERE ARE MANY WAYS to structure your time, space, and finances in order to minister incarnationally. Tuning the parameters of your ministry to something that you can sustain for the long term is a process that should involve prayer, humility, and flexibility. One approach may lead to frustration and burnout, while another leads to a fruitful ministry. The right ministry approach for you and your team is not the one that is most impressively ascetic or extreme, nor is it the one that seems the most comfortable or easiest to explain to your family. The right approach is the one that allows you to be meaningfully engaged in your community for the long haul.

Ultimately, the decision regarding an incarnational approach should not be an individual one. All of the members of the team need to be able to support each other's approach, even if the best option is to have a variety of approaches within one team. The local residents must also accept and be blessed by the team's approach. Finally, the minister must be flexible enough to re-examine the approach if it is not working well over time.

Let's explore approaches by first looking at two options for household income: living at the poverty level of the neighborhood, or living above it. Then, we will look at a handful of models for where to live and how to divide time in relation to the community.

Living at the Poverty Level

When I first lived in an urban poor community, the only approach to incarnational ministry which I was aware of was living at the poverty level of my average urban poor neighbor. I originally understood that living among the urban poor was all about experiencing life exactly as they did. I assumed that if you were not living at the level of the average squatter in the community, you were somehow not incarnational.

I had a massive rat infestation but refused to actually fix the holes to prevent the rats from coming in, because all of my neighbors also had rat problems. My clothes had holes in them. I ate street food alongside the poor. Inside my home was a small stove, eating utensils, a light, a fan, a sheet, a pillow, and several changes of clothes that I kept in a suitcase. That was about it. I lived like this for about ten months. I lived so simply that several people in the community thought I was just as poor as everyone else in the neighborhood. Considering that urban poor Filipinos tend to assume that all Americans are wealthy, I must have been living extremely simply for them to consider me poor.

This approach stresses learning from the community, and it may be very valuable during the first phase of a ministry journey. The first several months will immerse the leader in many new experiences, and the leader can learn a lot by embracing poverty as fully as possible. However, there comes a point when the experiences are no longer new. Carrying water in buckets helped me to fully realize just how heavy water can be and how much time it takes to carry it. It has also helped me learn how to conserve water. Yet I do not need to carry water in buckets for the rest of my life to retain this lesson.

One problem with this model is that the poor are not impressed by others becoming destitute. Living at the exact level of poverty of urban poor neighbors would mean refusing to seek needed medical care for yourself or even your children because the urban poor cannot afford specialized treatment. When incarnational leaders die from preventable illness, many years of ministry are wasted. Their neighbors might also think that they were foolish or wasteful for not using the resources that they had. If this happens to a child who is denied care, the urban poor may conclude that the leaders are immorally neglectful as parents.

Living at the level of poverty of the urban poor takes a great deal of time. It takes time to do everything by hand, like washing dishes and clothes. For the urban poor in the United States, taking clothes to a laundromat requires lugging clothes across town and back, after waiting hours for them to finish. It can take two to three times longer to get places taking public transportation as opposed to driving a private car. Living at the level of the poor can eat up all of our time and energy, leaving little room to work for the transformation of the community. Ministry can certainly take place while waiting in a laundromat and on public transportation, so these should not be written off in the name of efficiency. But we must acknowledge that there is real a cost in terms of time and energy.

In some urban poor communities, becoming as poor as the residents is simply not feasible. Particularly in new squatter communities or refugee camps, the situation may be so destitute that relief from the outside is more appropriate than living within the community. Even within established communities, some families always worry about not having enough to eat, or how to pay for medical bills. It is extremely hard to think of others when our own basic needs are not met. This is considered destitute poverty. In almost all cases, living at the level of poverty of the urban poor should not be taken to this extreme for any length of time.

Pause and Reflect:

1. What are the advantages of living at the poverty level?
2. What are the disadvantages?
3. In what ways might this approach come into play in your ministry? How can you support or collaborate with those who use this approach?

Living above the Poverty Level

Living above the poverty level of the poor could range from living slightly to significantly above the lifestyle of your average urban poor neighbor. It is more than possible to live meaningfully in the community at a lifestyle that is above the level of the average neighbor. This approach stresses being present in the community. It recognizes that families and those with unique needs can have powerful ministries among the urban poor without neglecting their own well-being.

After burning out in attempts to live at the level of poverty of the urban poor, I began to shift my thinking about incarnational ministry. It became more about being present in the community than about replicating the poverty of the urban poor.[62] This has been a slow process and has come as a result of life changes such as getting married, having a child, and aging. We have also realized that being hospitable and generous is integral to our ministry, so we make sure we have enough to share with others. As discussed in chapter four, we also find it appropriate to seek quality health care for ourselves and our children, and we find creative ways to connect our community to these services as well.

These decisions do not alienate us from our communities, as we intentionally share and relate across our privilege rather than hoarding it. In many ways we are socially, economically, and educationally well above our neighbors. Educationally, we both hold advanced degrees. With our salary from Servant Partners, we are in the upper ten percent as far as monthly income in our community. We are not, however, the top earner. Believe it or not, an American family living in a squatter area in Manila actually earns less monthly than some of the local families. Every community is socioeconomically diverse, and we don't need to be at the very bottom in order to be a good neighbor.

I realize there are some incarnational leaders who live a bit more extravagantly than what I would choose. They may need to consider a simpler lifestyle, particularly if they are becoming a stumbling block for others in the community. Likewise, those taking the "how low can you go" approach may need to consider the validity of living at a higher standard than others in the community.

With the focus on being present in the community, one is free to live at a level above the average urban poor family. At its worst, this method might allow the leader to slip into indulgence and isolation from the pains of poverty. But at its best, this approach balances being present in the community with a sustainable lifestyle.

Pause and Reflect:

1. What are the advantages of living above the poverty level?
2. What are the disadvantages?
3. In what ways might this approach come into play in your ministry? How can you support or collaborate with those who use this approach?

Living on the Edge of the Community

In some special circumstances, it is viable to live in a middle-class neighborhood on the edge of an urban poor community. This means the incarnational leader is not living directly among the urban poor, but may still be close enough to be connected. This is sometimes necessary in situations where the urban poor community is made up of subsidized housing with a waiting list, or when it is just not possible to find an available place to rent. This might also be a viable compromise when some family members have a stronger sense of calling than others.

By default, this was how we lived our last few years in Balic-Balic. We wanted to live directly in the squatter community, but after several months of looking for a place to rent within the boundaries of the church's outreach, we were unsuccessful. The choice was between renting a squatter home along the train tracks a significant distance from the church, or renting a middle-class apartment that was a one-minute walk from the neighborhood. Since we had already spent significant time living in squatter communities, we decided it was more important to be physically present than to live in a similar house. There were several advantages, comfort-wise, to being off the tracks. We did not have the dust and noise from the train interrupting us all the time. Every evening, the train tracks practically became a street party since so many people were out. Living off the tracks allowed us to hang out on the tracks as long as we wanted and then return to our place, which was usually quieter—except when our neighbor played his stereo at full volume and yelled at his family when he was drunk.

I felt unnecessary guilt about this decision. At the time, I did not have a category for incarnational ministry that did not involve living directly in a squatter community. Our home was about the same size of a squatter home, and not much nicer. In fact, some of our church members who were extremely poor also rented in the surrounding area and not directly in the squatter community. But I still wanted to be in the neighborhood. It is only in hindsight that I can fully appreciate the wisdom of the decision to be physically close. We still lived simply, so our church friends still felt comfortable in our house. We used our home for children's Vacation Bible School, as well as occasional Bible studies. It is more than possible to have a powerful ministry with this kind of approach.

If the urban poor community is isolated or the neighboring areas are significantly wealthier, this approach is simply not an option. It can also lead to pursuing a middle-class lifestyle. The discipline of simplicity is just as important, and maybe more so, in a middle-class home.

This approach can also cause some social tension. We know a family who lives in the last apartment in a middle-class district bordering a squatter community. This created some difficulty for their children. The middle-class kids did not want to interact with their children because they saw them going into the urban poor community. They were also not fully accepted by the urban poor children. As a family, they never found a solution. Their children were outsiders everywhere. Within this tension, it is important to pray for peace either by finding a more settled solution or by coming to terms with the tension.

If you already live in a middle-class community near the urban poor, be encouraged that you can begin ministering with your nearby neighbors now. However, remember to stay open to the possibility that God may call you even closer.

Pause and Reflect:

1. What are the advantages of living on the edge of the community?
2. What are the disadvantages?
3. In what ways might this approach come into play in your ministry? How can you support or collaborate with those who use this approach?

Living with a Local Family

I only have limited experience living with a family in an urban poor community. My first three months of urban poor ministry consisted of commuting to Balic-Balic on Saturday morning and leaving on Monday morning. While I was there, I stayed with Pastor Ronnel and his mother, who everyone called Mama. They were not from that specific community; they were there because it was Pastor Ronnel's first pastorate. It was truly a blessing to be welcomed to stay in their small home each weekend.

As an initial entry point in the community, language and culture learning is much easier this way. I learned many valuable cultural lessons during those first few months of living with Pastor Ronnel. It also provides a natural way to meet the family's friends. Living with a family allows for a unique view of life that would not happen in any other way than through regularly sleeping in the same house and sharing the same space. This is more than just sleeping over for a weekend. It includes seeing how families cope with difficulties and experiencing how they celebrate accomplishments and holidays.

Safety is another potential advantage. Living with a family allows for more people to be in the house more often, limiting the chances of someone breaking in. The flip side of this, of course, is the lack of personal space and time alone for reflection. When families lack awareness of cross-cultural issues, leaders can feel as if they are always being judged, even for things they have no control over such as their skin color or weight. It can also be stressful for the family that you are staying with. During every disagreement or complication, they have a guest in the house watching it all.

While living with a family allows us to bond with the family on the one hand, it may limit bonding with the community on the other. We can learn from one family, but this family may or may not have a lifestyle that is typical of the neighborhood. You may also be caught up in any conflicts or reputations the family has in the neighborhood. Generally, urban poor families that have the space to host someone are in the upper strata of the community. If there is a sharp divide between the poorest and wealthiest residents, by default the incarnational leader will be perceived as siding with the wealthiest.

Another disadvantage of living with a family is that one can be sheltered from some of the responsibilities of surviving in the neighborhood. When I lived with an urban poor family, I never learned how to shop in the market or cook because Mama insisted that these were her roles. Living with a family can also limit the incarnational leader's ability to host neighbors, making it difficult to be hospitable.

Generally, living with a family is a temporary situation. It is not a sustainable approach to long-term incarnational ministry unless the living space is slightly separated, such as renting a room or back house without becoming a member of the family. This helps to eliminate the risk of getting caught up in family conflict or being severely limited in your ministry due to the family's demands on your time or misalignment of values. However, the family should have a source of income other than the rent money the incarnational leader will pay.

There may be situations where it is sustainable to live with a family long term. A single woman in a strict Muslim country may have to live with a family so she is not seen as immoral, for example. Knowing your context will be important at this point. The arrangement should probably be given a trial period. For example, you and your host can have a three-month agreement followed by an evaluation to see if the situation is a good fit for everyone involved. Though difficult, God can work out a family hosting situation for good. Prayer and discernment will need to go into choosing a family.

Having urban poor housemates is another option that is similar to living with a family. Much of the same dynamics that arise from living with a family are relevant for housemates. While this can also be difficult in the long term, under certain circumstances it can work.

Pause and Reflect:

1. What are the advantages of living with an urban poor family?
2. What are the disadvantages?
3. In what ways might this approach come into play in your ministry? How can you support or collaborate with those who use this approach?

The 50/50 Approach

The 50/50 approach is when an incarnational leader lives both inside and outside of the community. My first three months in urban poor ministry were essentially the 50/50 approach.

I would spend Saturday morning to Monday morning in the squatter neighborhood and the rest of the time in middle-class housing near where I attended school.

This approach is part of the journey for many, particularly for students and those with families. It is generally not a planned approach; rather, it is the incarnational leader taking baby steps as God slowly opens his or her eyes to urban poverty. The incarnational leader may be drawn to the community, but for a wide variety of reasons is not ready, or perhaps able, to move all the way in. For me, it was because I was a student. For others, it might be because they have family commitments or because their spouse is not yet fully on board with moving into an urban poor context.

Trying this approach provides room for God to continue his work in the life of incarnational leaders before calling them to fully relocate. This can be potentially beneficial for both the incarnational leader and the community. The incarnational leader is able to get a feel for urban poor life and is able to learn about living meaningfully and engaging the community for transformation before making a more permanent commitment to the neighborhood.

The 50/50 approach is limited in that it does not fully connect the leader to the community. In fact, the perception that the leader is rich enough to have two homes could further alienate the community. It should not be misunderstood as a justification for spending a small fraction of the week in the community. If the only time spent in the neighborhood is for planned church or community activities, this is not the 50/50 approach at all.

Pause and Reflect:

1. What are the advantages of the 50/50 approach?
2. What are the disadvantages?
3. In what ways might this approach come into play in your ministry? How can you support or collaborate with those who use this approach?

Intentional Community

One approach that is gaining popularity is the development of intentional Christian community. The basis of this movement is the example set by the early Christians in Acts, who held all things in common as they ministered.[63] There are numerous models, purposes, and even definitions of intentional community. For our purposes, I will define it as a group of Christians living together in the same house for the purpose of ministry, since this is the most dominant model. Living in separate apartments while sharing communal meals is another potential model, but it will not be discussed here.

My experience of intentional community has always been temporary, so I cannot speak about it with much authority. However, my friend John, who lived in an ultimately unsuccessful community in Canada, shared his experience with me.[64] He cited a lack of vision and commitment among his housemates as a major reason for the community's failure. He believes they could have been successful if they had done three things differently. First, they should have had a strong, solidified vision before starting so that they could support and encourage each other toward it. Second, they should have worked through all of the details, such as who would purchase groceries, who would do chores, and who was in charge of group devotions, to make sure that these things happened consistently and no resentments grew. Third, they would have benefited from an outside group that would serve as something like an advisory board for the house. This would have provided much-needed accountability and support.

Intentional communities have the risk of becoming overly inward-focused. Neighborhood ministry can fade into the background as the intentional community focuses on itself and becomes a convent that just happens to be located in an urban poor neighborhood. An intentional outward focus, supported by strong internal and external accountability, can help to prevent this.

Living in intentional community has many potential benefits for incarnational ministry among the urban poor. However, it also has its own unique set of challenges that need to be overcome. Some will flourish in this kind of environment, while others will struggle.

Pause and Reflect:

1. What are the advantages of living in intentional community?
2. What are the disadvantages?
3. In what ways might this approach come into play in your ministry? How can you support or collaborate with those who use this approach?

Commuter Ministries: A Last Resort

Visiting urban poor communities is of course not a bad thing to do. However, it is a less effective way to minister, as it severely limits the extent to which a leader can be said to be incarnational. The leader who simply can't live in his or her ministering community must put in a lot of effort to overcome the sense of artificial engagement and other strong social barriers that are caused by driving home to a relatively wealthy community each night.

If I speak strongly about the dangers of commuter ministries, it's only because I know how unhelpful and humiliating it can be when a well-meaning outsider tries to diagnose and fix your problems for you. Though I've seen this happen many times since, I still think back to the day in eleventh grade when my nose began to bleed in front of the substitute teacher. He came in the hall with me and asked me a lot of questions, after which he came to the conclusion that my nose was always bleeding because I was sniffing drugs. He sent me to the office. In his mind, he becomes the hero because he saved some kid from a lifetime of addiction. In reality, my nose bled because of an old sports injury, but he thought he knew my problem more than I knew my own problem. I will always remember this story in my work among the urban poor, as this type of intervention is the opposite of incarnational ministry.

Though I obviously do not recommend commuter ministries and the mindset that too often comes with them, there are occasions when it is simply not financially feasible for someone to move into the urban poor community where he or she ministers. In Manila, this is one of the hindrances to Filipinos relocating into the urban poor community, especially those Filipino seminary students who are working toward a Masters in Transformational Urban Leadership. Many of them live with their families. They are able to stay for free and in many cases do not have to help contribute to food and other expenses. The money they spend on transportation to commute to where they minister is minimal in comparison to how much it would cost for them to rent a room in a squatter community. In these cases, a person can intentionally work to develop an incarnational presence through consistency and relationship building, and by serving in partnership with those who do have an incarnational presence in the neighborhood.

Pastor Carlos, who is at Church of the Redeemer in South Los Angeles, cannot move into the community where his church is located because his family cannot afford rent in the immediate area of the church. He has been in his current apartment for seventeen years. With Los Angeles rent control laws, his family is paying significantly less for their monthly rent than they would pay anywhere else. Even if they moved next door, they would have to pay much more. Space is also part of the issue; they are currently in a one-bedroom apartment with their four children. They do not want to move until they can afford a two-bedroom apartment.[65]

It may also be difficult to live among a destitute population such as a refugee camp, homeless colony, or on skid row. There are quite a few Christians who choose to sleep out on the streets with their homeless friends from time to time. The leaders of one ministry among street children bring cardboard boxes to sleep in their street community several times a week. But long-term sustainability is extremely difficult in these situations, and it may be more sustainable to minister to these populations while maintaining or modifying your current living situation.

When commuter ministries are necessary, there is usually a way to push them toward either an on-the-edge or 50/50 approach by being in the community as much and as meaningfully as possible. Selecting important non-church community celebrations to attend, as well as being available to meet with church members in times of crisis, can help you to have a more significant place in the life of the community. If you live so far away from your site that you cannot be meaningfully present outside of ministry program hours, you may want to consider moving either your home or your ministry.

Pause and Reflect:

1. What are the advantages of commuting to your site?
2. What are the disadvantages?
3. In what ways might this approach come into play in your ministry? How can you support or collaborate with those who use this approach?

Conclusion

Knowing yourself, your ministry, and your context will help you determine an appropriate approach to living among the urban poor. Whether or not to live at the poverty line, whether or not to live in the community full time, and whether to live alone or with others are key questions that will shape the development of a ministry. Though less desirable, there are sometimes instances where residence is not an option, and a commuter ministry can be approached with an incarnational mindset instead. While approaches change over time and there is no one right way for everyone in every context, discerning an appropriate approach can greatly eliminate unnecessary stress and open doors for deep personal and community transformation.

---

[62] Review "Love at the Center" in Chapter 2 for reflections on the role of the material in building relationships with the poor.

[63] Acts 2:42-47

[64] Interview with "John," June 24, 2011. Quezon City, Philippines.

[65] Interview with Pastor Carlos De La Rocha, July 6, 2011. Los Angeles, CA.

12

CHOOSING A LOCATION

WITH TODAY'S ONE BILLION SLUM RESIDENTS living in urban centers all around the globe, it may feel like there are an infinite number of potential communities where one might minister. Narrowing down the nation, people group, or city where you might minister should be based on prayer, the advice of trusted mentors, need and opportunity, and our God-given passions.

Sometimes your church or sending organization will identify a location with or for you, based on the current status of their programming at various locations. Other times, you may have a good idea of where you want to relocate before you even approach your sending organization, or you may develop a strong preference as you explore your options. The key is to take one step at a time and not to stress too much about it. If we don't find our ministry home the first time, God will not abandon us. We need to trust him to guide us where he wants us to serve, recognizing that we might have to adjust some of our plans based on how God is working.

A warning here is important: problems, difficulties, and struggles are not signs that you are in the wrong place. In urban poor ministry, these are the daily reality. Sustaining a ministry in a single location won't be based on finding a location where everything instantly clicks. It can take years for the fruit of ministry to appear, even in a place that is a good fit.

Community-Specific Features

While most urban poor communities have some key things in common, they are nowhere close to identical. Factors such as culture, language, distance from your family, political atmosphere, and religious landscape will deeply affect your experience and the shape of your ministry. All of these factors should be considered in light of who you are and the role you feel led to play in the context of the community. For example, your gender may limit the types of relationships and ministries you can develop in certain locations. Knowing the language may give you a head start on integrating with the community, while being a language learner could provide an explanation for your presence.

The specific community dynamics will determine which of the approaches from chapter eleven are even possible. The railroad squatter community of Balic-Balic was located in the heart of the city. In the densely packed urban environment, it was hard to tell where the squatter community ended and the legal housing started. This allowed us to live in middle-class housing on the edge of the squatter community, which was a blessing to us as new parents.

This is not the case for every community. Sunrise is a squatter community located on the outer edge of Manila. It borders Laguna Lake on one side and a factory on the other. There is nothing else around because the area is being used as an unofficial dumpsite. Unlike Balic-Balic, there are no surrounding houses. There is no option to live just outside the community. Either you live in Sunrise or you commute to get there. The unique features of the community will need to be considered when discerning the best incarnational approach.

The infrastructure of a community is another important consideration. If the community lacks water and electricity, this will make it especially difficult for a family with children. After Balic-Balic, we considered moving to a community located directly on Laguna Lake. The homes were all makeshift wooden structures on stilts. There was no running water or electricity. At that time, Zach was only a few months old. After praying and talking with mentors, we determined moving to this community was not the best idea.

Ultimately, if God is directing you to a location, any external factor can be worked through. Cultural and language can be learned, family issues can be sorted out, families can adapt to a gap in resources, and the political and religious landscape can be worked around. But part of your discernment process should involve exploring locations that can provide a good fit for you and your family.

Pause and Reflect:

1. What nation, people group, or specific city, if any, have you experienced a draw toward in the past?
2. Are you drawn to live among the poorest of the poor, or do you require a community with a basic level of infrastructure?
3. Write out your thoughts on some key factors: Is distance from home an important factor? What about language? Are you comfortable representing Christianity as a minority or illegal religion? How densely packed and urban an environment do you think you will live in?

Insider/Outsider Status

Both insider and outsider status have their advantages in ministry. Insiders have more knowledge of the community and may not have to work as hard to establish trust and connection. Outsiders are more likely to be noticed and can make a fresh impression on the community. The extent to which you fit in or stand out will be one aspect to consider as you think about potential locations.

There can be many points of connection or disconnection with your community, such as language, culture, race, ethnicity, economic background, hobbies, interests, religious background, and values. It is likely that you will be considered an insider in some ways and an outsider in others. Let's look at two key metrics that can cause you to be seen as either an insider or an outsider.

LOCAL OR RELOCATED? Incarnational ministry does not always involve relocating into a distant urban poor community. It does not even necessarily require moving at all. God may be raising you up to minister within your own community. Indigenous incarnational leaders are those followers of Jesus who choose to stay in their communities in order to minister incarnationally, as well as those who are bound to stay by their poverty but choose to live incarnationally while they are there.

Alvaro Barreiro writes about Basic Ecclesial Communities, a grassroots movement among poor Catholics in Brazil who "desire to live in accordance with the demands of the gospel."[66] These local incarnational leaders are living meaningfully in their communities and are able to effectively evangelize among their neighbors. I would add to Barreiro's emphasis on local leadership that collaboration with relocated leaders of other classes is also important.

Ema was an indigenous incarnational minister for about five years when we returned to Balic-Balic. We stayed in that community until it was demolished in 2008. Overall, Ema was welcomed back, although there was some confusion as to why she was choosing to live in a squatter community instead of the United States. While this provided opportunities to share about Jesus, some in the neighborhood could not understand her decision.

I do not have any personal experience as an indigenous incarnational leader. In fact, I never will. Even if I moved back to the home where I grew up, I could not be an indigenous incarnational leader because the demographics of my old neighborhood have changed so much. I would probably only know a few of the neighbors, so I would still be coming in as an outsider. However, having worked with many indigenous leaders in Manila, I have seen firsthand how incredibly valuable their insider perspective and deep roots are to God's movements within their community.

INTER- AND INTRA-ETHNIC MINISTRIES. One consideration in choosing where to minister is how someone from your race, ethnicity, and nationality will be viewed in each location. For example, the urban poor in Manila may be confused that white Americans would live in their community because it is assumed that they could live in a wealthy subdivision instead. They might be viewed negatively, perhaps as a pedophile or as someone looking for a prostitute. When we first moved to Botocan, we tried to live simply and honestly in order to overcome these stereotypes.

Alternately, white westerners may be praised or put into positions of church leadership simply because they are white. Counteracting this internalized racism can take an exhausting intentionality, and may never be fully effective. On the other hand, an Asian American living in the same community may simply be ignored. It is frustrating and painful to see white teammates being elevated into leadership positions at your expense because of their race.

When the incarnational leader is of the same the same race/ ethnicity as the community but was raised in a different cultural background, specific concerns arise. Julie's parents were immigrants from India who raised her fully in the United States. She shared the painful story of her experience ministering in India, and she hopes that her experience helps others.[67]

Julie realized immediately after arriving that she would be treated differently than her other teammates. When she first went to the community, her team leader showed them around and introduced them to people in the neighborhood. The community residents were much more interested in meeting her white teammates. She had a hard time finding a language helper, and the community members even criticized her for not being fluent already. Churches would ask her white teammates to teach or lead, but she would be ignored. Women in the churches would approach her white husband and talk to him, sometimes even flirtatiously, as she stood by his side. Julie was trying to do the same things as her teammates, but she was not getting the same response. She did not feel satisfied in her role and did not have a fulfilling ministry.

The white Americans on her team did not understand what Julie was going through. She felt there was no intentionality in bringing her into leadership. She wanted to be an example of someone of her ethnicity in church leadership, but she was not ever afforded the opportunity. Eventually she realized that people simply did not know how to fit her into their existing categories. She also realized that most mission training is not developed for workers who are ethnically similar but culturally different.

Julie later shared her thoughts on what might have made her ministry more sustainable. Her mission organization had a policy that the first two years in the field would be for language and culture learning. However, local residents did not have a category for someone who looked like them trying to learn the language. Any role or job other than language learner would help to provide the community with a category for her and may have allowed her to secure opportunities for leadership despite the trend toward elevating white teammates.

Pause and Reflect:

1. Are you generally comfortable as an outsider, or do you prefer to live in spaces where you are an insider?
2. Do you feel any draw to minister in the community where you were raised? Why or why not?
3. Do you feel any draw to minister in the region of your family's heritage? Why or why not?

Visiting Potential Communities

We do not have to move into a community totally blind. Spying out the land or doing our homework before moving in can spare us unnecessary stress and help us to have a more effective ministry. We might not be able to know exactly who our neighbors will be, but we can at least know the general area and the possibilities for ministry that come with it. In order to illustrate my point, let's take a tour of my current setting, Botocan, and compare it with an urban poor community in South Los Angeles.

BOTOCAN TOUR. Located at the bottom of a small hill, lower Botocan is on the edge of a middle-class community. This area is a short walk to public transportation and is accessible without having to pay extra for special trips on tricycles. It is also close to the market, which makes it a more desirable location. The result is that rent prices tend to be higher in this part of Botocan. The downside to living in this part of Botocan is that since it is at the bottom of the hill, it tends to flood during heavy rains.

We live in the central area of Botocan. This area is higher up, so we do not experience flooding even during the major storms that have caused extensive damage in other areas of Manila. However, being deeper inside the community makes things less accessible. To carry things such as groceries home requires either walking through town with heavy bags or paying triple the cost for a special trip on a tricycle (a motorcycle with a sidecar for transporting passengers). The middle of Botocan is also where the main basketball court is located. This is where all neighborhood activities are held. Those of us living near the basketball court can hear everything that is happening. This means when there are late night dance parties and singing contests, we are often kept awake until early morning. We have also been awakened in the early morning by dance music when the basketball court is being used for exercise.

The upper part of Botocan is the most isolated, but there is a side entrance that allows access from another neighboring middle-class community. Residents carrying groceries have no choice but to walk because even if they pay for a special trip, most tricycle drivers do not like to go past the basketball court. There is a smaller market in this area, but the prices are generally higher than the larger market in lower Botocan. So although this area is free from flooding, residents have to pay more for special trips or walk farther.

SOUTH LOS ANGELES TOUR. Elliot, an incarnational minister at The Church of the Redeemer in South Los Angeles,[68] describes the surrounding community as follows: the church is in the center of a neighborhood that occupies about one square mile. Its boundaries are major roads and the University of Southern California (USC). There are three grocery stores located in this area. Most of the other businesses there are smaller specialty shops, so shopping for everyday household items often involves traveling.

One of the primary social issues in South Los Angeles is racial tension, so evaluating a neighborhood in South Los Angeles should always involve considerations of racial dynamics. The residents are mainly Latinos and African Americans. In general, there is a greater concentration of Latinos in the north of the neighborhood and more of an even mix in the south.

The northwest area is mostly single-family homes. There are more homeowners, which means the turnover rate is less than the rental areas. There is a park that is used for community activities. The population is African American and second generation Latino, so learning Spanish is not necessary to connect with neighbors. This area is experiencing some gentrification, which might eventually cause the urban poor population to be pushed out. This sector borders a main road which caters to prostitution and is not without either crime or ministry need. The northeast area is in the territory known for shootings and gang-related violence. Residents in this section are at risk of being caught up in the crossfire. Yet it also offers significant opportunities for youth ministry.

The southeast area has USC's influence and is home to many student renters. This relatively wealthy and transient population is generally not an appropriate focus for urban poor ministry, though living near university housing could provide the opportunity to bridge college students with their urban poor neighbors. The southwest area is mostly made up of single-family homes. The only local library is in this area, as well as a family park and elementary school. Living here may help with family life, as a walk to the park or library is feasible. It is farther away from USC, so there are more permanent residents with whom one can build relationships.

Regardless of the specific area, the population density of the street makes a huge difference. The less densely populated areas are usually blocks with mostly single-family homes. These tend to be quieter and more stable, since families generally stay longer. The residents are often more relationally open and less afraid of their community. The more densely populated blocks are made up mostly of renters. Renters are usually more transient, so it's harder to establish long-term ministries. These areas also tend to be louder and more prone to crime.

Pause and Reflect:

1. What similarities and contrasts did you notice between Botocan and East Los Angeles?
2. In the style of these tours, how would you describe your current home community?
3. What elements stand out as ones that you should look for as you visit potential communities?

Choosing Your Home

In certain communities, it is possible to find a home without any contacts or knowledge of the specific area. However, it is not safe to assume that you will be able to do so successfully. When Ema and I returned to Balic-Balic with Servant Partners, we spent two months in temporary housing while looking for a home. This temporary house, which was slightly off the train tracks, did not have running water. The walls also leaked, so every time it rained we would have puddles downstairs. Toward the end of the rainy season, we finally found another, more livable home.

In Botocan, we were able to meet a few people through our relationship with our new partner church before relocating. We ended up renting a ground floor house with plans to turn the second floor into our new church. After living in the community for several months, we discovered we lived in what was considered to be the most dangerous section of Botocan. Although our home is not the best in terms of limiting stress, it is in a great location which fits both of our personalities. We live directly on a major walkway, which means that Ema and I can meet people without much effort—which is perfect, as we are both introverts. It has also been good for Zach, since his friends can come over all the time. By having him play at home, we are able to supervise his activities.

Choosing the right home may also include deciding whether to buy or to rent. In many urban poor communities, buying or renting is not an issue because these communities are comprised of only rental units. However, in some urban poor communities, there is the option to purchase a home. Buying can be beneficial in helping the incarnational leader have a sense of permanence. However, if there is a sharp divide between renters and owners, purchasing a home could alienate you from the renters, who are generally less wealthy.

Pause and Reflect:

1. What bare-minimum standards do you have for your new home?
2. Do you see your home as a ministry hub or a quiet sanctuary? How will this affect your housing choice?
3. Do your location and life circumstances push you toward buying or renting your home?

Conclusion

Having a sense that you are at home in your urban poor community is important for sustaining a ministry long term. The choice of where to live is one that comes through exposure, evaluating needs and opportunities, and being aware of how your insider/outsider dynamics might affect ministry in different places. Visiting and learning about potential communities will help you to make your location decision and also begin visioning ministry possibilities, as well as determining which part of town would be ideal and what housing is available there. Ultimately, any place can become home if you bring a long-haul mindset with you.

---

[66] Alvaro Barreiro, *Basic Ecclesial Communities: The Evangelization of the Poor*, trans. Barbara Campbell (Maryknoll, NY: Orbis Books, 1984), 28.
[67] Interview with "Julie," August 8, 2011. Indian Wells, CA.
[68] Interview with Elliot Ling, August 16, 2011. Los Angeles, CA.

13

ENGAGEMENT AND DISENGAGEMENT

LIVING AMONG THE URBAN POOR for an extended period of time is difficult. Those who feel called to this ministry must develop sustainable habits and patterns which can be maintained for a lifetime. We simply cannot be "on," in ministry mode, every hour of the day and every day of the year. Engagement needs to go hand in hand with disengagement. Disengagement includes maintaining boundaries on your level of engagement, as well as taking time for reflection, spiritual activity, and self-care.

Disengagement is harder than it sounds. Urban ministers tend to be people of action. It takes discipline to choose disengagement when there is a never-ending list of needs and possibilities. While it feels like we are taking time away from our ministry when we limit engagement, we must remember that we are in fact adding many healthy, effective years to it.

Boundaries

Relational boundaries are important in all human relationships. However, they are pushed to center stage when living in urban poor communities. We relocate because we want to be among the poor, and that means our boundaries are always tested.

The worst thing to do would be to start out with no boundaries, only to snap one day because of the overwhelming amount of stress. The simplest boundary that all ministers should practice is saying "no" when we are asked to engage beyond our capacity, and trying not to volunteer for more commitments than we can realistically maintain. We also need to maintain the physical boundary of shutting our door when we need personal space, counter-cultural as it may be.

Since our home is also our ministry hub, we have had to set limits regarding how late kids and youth can stay at our home in the evening. In addition to protecting our sleep, this is part of our effort not to take over too many of the practical or emotional roles of these children's parents—at least not at the expense of parents who are able to fill them. While we generally rejoice in an emotional intimacy with our neighbors that is well above the western average, Ema and I also choose to avoid complications by limiting the intimacy of one-on-one conversations with neighbors of the opposite gender.

As discussed in chapter five, we hope to hold generosity as a central value. We understand our home and possessions to be at the service of the community. However, we do have boundaries around non-reciprocal gifts, especially financial gifts that can cause dependence and dehumanize relationships. Though it is tempting (and sometimes good and necessary) to step in to relieve others' needs, we always try to pause and look for ways to help others grow stronger and less dependent.

The act of moving into an urban poor community removes the physical boundary of distance that previously existed between you and the urban poor, and new boundaries are needed in response. Balanced with a generous, genuine value for human interaction, boundaries can increase the quality of your relationships and help both you and your neighbors to feel respected.

Pause and Reflect:

1. Describe a time when you struggled to maintain a healthy boundary, in ministry or otherwise.
2. What sorts of boundaries do you hold in your current relationships?
3. Is it difficult for you to say "no" when you are asked to help beyond your capacity?

Action/Reflection

Community organizer Robert Linthicum shared that "for every minute spent in action, a minute should be spent in reflection."[69] This means we must take the time to evaluate our ministries, rather than carrying out programs and making decisions on autopilot. The process of reflecting allows incarnational leaders to grow and to work more effectively for the transformation of a community.

Our partner church in Manila, Faith Gospel Community, is a great example of an urban poor church that has integrated action/ reflection in the life of their church. Immediately after their youth service, the leaders have a formal evaluation meeting. The results of the evaluation are integrated into the next service. At BBCF, we aspire to reflect so regularly and sincerely, but it is still a struggle!

The longer I minister, the more sharply I recognize that incarnational leaders can be dangerous characters. There are many ways in which a ministry can become detrimental, and it takes intention to become part of the solution, not the problem. Slipping into negative or unhealthy ways of being can lead to frustration, resentment, and burnout, and I have even heard of a few ministers who have caused so much damage that they have had to move out for both their health and the health of the community. A thorough ministry evaluation will look honestly at both intentions and their outcomes and will adjust them for long-term success and relational health in the community. Evaluation is always a messy and imperfect process, but I want to list a few red flags that we try to look out for at BBCF.

First, we honestly ask whether our programs and personal actions aim to diagnose and correct our neighbors and their problems instead of sitting with them in their suffering. Like the friends who visited Job in his grief,[70] we can come in empathy and love only to restlessly decide that we need to do something—even something that is not necessary and in fact antagonizes the poor themselves.

We also need to ask whether our engagement is empowering, or whether it reinforces imbalances. Some use ministry to satisfy their desire to feel important and needed. To curb this impulse, we keep a central rule in leadership that we do not do for others what they are capable of doing for themselves, even if this leaves us with an unimpressive amount of things to do. This is one reason why I do not favor feeding programs in non-destitute urban poor communities. The funds would be better spent on other forms of assistance that contribute to long-term empowerment.

We also ask whether we are trying to cheat on the long, hard, uphill journey of ministry among the urban poor. Are we trying to settle for cheap external victories, such as using social pressure to get members to imitate behaviors we have decided are Christian? Are we taking the time to celebrate small genuine victories, such as the youth reducing their daily video game use from twelve hours to five hours and engaging in the community instead?

Finally, we ask if our programs are understood and well received in our communities. As I have mentioned before, one-on-one discipleship is no longer a central part of our church programming. The communal culture of Manila means that church members thrive in group discussion. Though the occasional shy resident might appreciate the option, one-on-one discipleship may seem inappropriately exclusive and isolating to the average Filipino/a, who might prefer to invite his or her friends to these meetings.

Being critical of programs and their outcomes will help to determine whether activities are actually necessary, empowering, genuine, and culturally appropriate. Wishing to do good is not enough. We need to take the time to reflect on whether we actually are doing good.

Pause and Reflect:

1. Which of these evaluation points resonate with your current ministry or community engagement?
2. How do you think you would respond if a co-leader told you that your actions were causing problems in one of these areas?
3. What metric of evaluation would you add to this partial list of evaluation criteria?

Spiritual Disciplines

The inner character of the incarnational leader is vital from the start. Living in an urban poor community, we have to be able to connect with God in the midst of noise, violence, and pain if we are to grow spiritually. Spiritual disciplines are practices for intentionally encountering and listening to God as part of our regular rhythms of life.

The Bible and church history give us a wide variety of spiritual disciplines. Your denomination may emphasize some, while others may be new to you. I recommend learning about and trying new disciplines to find the pattern which works for you. Your pattern should probably include Sabbaths, retreats, daily devotionals, and communal gatherings, along with other disciplines that you find meaningful.

SABBATHS. The essence of a Sabbath is life-giving rest. For some, this means spending one night per week at a guesthouse or retreat center. For others, it might mean a day spent in nature or reading a humorous book. Sabbaths do not have to be expensive and can also happen at places that the poor can also go to, such as a nearby park.

Urban environments in general are not conducive for Sabbath rests. If an incarnational leader does not intentionally schedule in a Sabbath rest each week, it simply will not happen. Ema and I have found we cannot disconnect if we stay at home. Invariably, someone will come over. This is why we often enjoy a day away from the community on our Sabbath.

RETREATS. In the life of an incarnational leader, there also needs to be some form of extended disengagement for rest and reflection. Spiritual retreats outside the city are important and give us a chance to enjoy the beauty of God's creation.[71] Retreats give us a break from the ugliness and pain within urban poor communities. They provide the space for reflecting on how God is working and for exploring new ways God might be at work. A one-year furlough back to your home of origin can also be a spiritual retreat.

The example of Christ affirms that we do not need to feel guilty for taking a break. In the midst of his compassion for the overwhelming needs of others, Jesus took several retreats to pray and reconnect with his Father during his three years of ministry.

DAILY DEVOTIONS. Having a daily devotional time with God can be a challenge in an urban poor environment. There is no single correct form, but a devotional time usually involves connecting with God through Scripture, reflective books, and possibly writing, song, or other forms of personal expression. I usually try to do this in the early morning before others wake up. This does not always happen because there are times when I am not able to go to bed early enough, or when a neighbor will wake up early and blast music for all the neighbors to hear. While it is important to actually schedule in a devotional time, we also need the flexibility to make adjustments when needed. Devotions are not homework assignments from God, and completing them should not be a stress-inducing task.

GATHERING WITH OTHER CHRISTIANS. By approaching spiritual growth communally, incarnational leaders are able to encourage others in their walk with God as they themselves are also encouraged. The close proximity of urban poor families can help to create an ideal environment for gathering consistently. While this is in itself a spiritual discipline, it also makes way for the communal practice of other disciplines.

Often, the Christians in Botocan teach us about growing closer to God as a community. They have group devotions every morning, meeting together for Bible reading and prayer. Every fourth Saturday of the month, all of the local believers are encouraged to fast from electronics to give more time for prayer. Creative applications of spiritual disciplines arise organically whenever believers gather to encourage each other in their faith.

Pause and Reflect:

1. What disciplines do your church and/or family emphasize?
2. What spiritual disciplines have you found to be most life-giving?
3. What is one new discipline you would like to integrate into your regular routines?

Health

There are two senses in which maintaining your health can be considered disengagement. First, concepts of health are cultural and might differ from your understanding of what is healthy. Therefore, seeking to be healthy based on your cultural understanding may seem like a departure from relating to the poor. Secondly, diet and exercise, as well as doctor visits, may take extra time, energy, money, and thought which might otherwise go to direct ministry. However, health is crucial both in these senses of disengagement, and also as a way to engage your neighbors in conversations about healthy action.

I am not a dietitian or a trained health worker, so I will not attempt to give any specific clinical advice here. Working with your doctor before and during your ministry will help you to determine your specific needs.

BALANCED DIET. Having a balanced diet is generally counter-cultural for the urban poor. For the short-term teams in Manila, we always have a "food of the poor" meal. This consists of the cheapest rice and some condiment such as soy sauce, ketchup, or just plain table salt. This meal is almost like fasting. We are hungry that day, but at least we do not feel sick to our stomachs. This would be a real risk if we chose to serve another accurate version of the 'food of the poor' meal—soft drinks and chips for breakfast, soft drinks and cookies for lunch, soft drinks and donuts for a snack, and soft drinks and candy bars for dinner. While this might be the regular diet of our urban poor neighbors, we as a family need to make wise decisions about our own diet in order to stay physically healthy.

It is understandable to have limited food choices for a two-week trip with a group. But for long-term urban poor ministry, we need to have greater control over our food. This may mean learning how to cook basic dishes or finding the best places to eat out. In Manila, the street food is inexpensive and usually good, but this may not be the case in every community. We also need to balance the cultural value of accepting hospitality with our own need for health. This might mean finding a polite way to decline unhealthy food, taking only a token amount of what is offered, and/or offering to host the meal more often.

Choosing a healthy diet also addresses the broader justice issue of food access. The basic economic principle of supply and demand comes into play. If more people bought carrots to snack on instead of chips, it would encourage farmers to plant more carrots, which then raises the supply and lowers the costs. This would allow the urban poor to buy even more carrots, while helping farmers to earn more money. Buying healthier food supports local healthy food industries in this small way.

EXERCISE. Lack of exercise opportunities is in many ways a cost of living among the urban poor. In addition to hectic schedules and lack of energy, weather and safety can be real impediments. In very polluted communities, the cons of outdoor exercise for health can even outweigh the pros. Finding time and space to exercise is important, but it may take some creativity.

Over the years, Ema and I have tried a variety of exercise routines, such as jumping rope or jogging at 4:00 a.m. with some local youth. As mentioned before, we started leading a group to the university every Saturday morning to play outdoor games. This has worked well, and it allows me to connect with others and have a devotional Bible study before we play. While one day a week is not ideal for exercise, it is better than nothing. Some may also choose to invest in a family gym membership to supplement their activity. While this may feel like a luxury to some, others may see it as a basic component of long-term health. In general, we should try to find ways to exercise with our neighbors as much as possible, as this engages the community toward health as well.

Pause and Reflect:

1. How much emphasis do you place on physical health? Why?
2. What goals do you have in terms of physical health as you minister?
3. What challenges does your chosen community present to your physical health?

Conclusion

In order to live in an urban poor context for a lifetime, the minister needs to live in a way that does not lead to burnout. This means taking time to rest and reflect, regularly practicing spiritual disciplines, and protecting your health and personal time and space. It is not selfish to meet your own basic needs, especially when it is done in a spirit of seeking the long-term health of the ministry.

[69] Interview with Robert Linthicum, August 9, 2011. Indian Wells, CA.
[70] Job 4 and following.
[71] Mark 1:35, 9:2, Luke 4:42, 5:16, 6:12, 9:28, and Matt. 14:13, 23

14

SEEING GOD EVERYWHERE

WHETHER YOU SPEND YOUR DAYS in an urban slum or in a high-rise office building, it is so easy to lose track of God's constant presence. Learning to see God everywhere, from the laughter of children to the pain of not having enough to eat, is essential. I close with these thoughts because they have done more to sustain my own ministry than any of the others, and I pray that you will carry them with you through many fruitful years among the urban poor as well.

A Theology of Suffering

It is important to have a strong theological understanding of suffering and struggle so that we do not lose sight of God in the midst of either. While some believers see suffering as evidence of a lack of faithfulness to God, nothing could be further from the truth. Some suffering may be directly caused by poor judgment, but this does not mean God vindictively punishes us for our mistakes. And it certainly doesn't mean that those who suffer are hiding terrible sins. We must remember this both when we experience hardship, and when we see the struggles of the poor.

We do not have all the answers to explain suffering, but we do know God is a good and loving God who willingly experienced suffering for our sake and is still with us in the midst of our pain. God calls us to seek him in prayer in the midst of pain, even crying out as the authors of the psalms so often did. Suffering needs to be seen as part of our faith. There needs to be a value for following the suffering Jesus in our lives—not to equate ourselves to him, but to be more willing to suffer for others and the Kingdom because of his example.

Because we are called to minister with our poor neighbors in their suffering, it can be difficult to value and process our own. We have to realistically acknowledge that our relative privilege protects us from some forms of suffering, but this does not mean that our own direct and empathetic pain are any less real. We do need to be thoughtful about how we choose to express suffering, especially to those who may be experiencing pain more directly. A good guideline is that we should process our traumas with those who are less directly affected by them than we are, rather than with someone who is more directly affected and probably needs a listening ear rather than more pain to process. All of us need to have a spouse, mentor, or counselor who will prayerfully listen to, affirm, and help us develop a Christlike response to our pain. We take on a lot of it as incarnational ministers, and it is okay to admit that we are hurting. Our suffering is real and it should not be minimized.

We also need to recognize that struggle is an important part of life. We need to struggle against our personal sins. We need to struggle with the physical hardships of urban poor life. We need to struggle with the emotional pain of our own brokenness and the brokenness of our neighbors. We need to struggle for the transformation of our communities. The reality is that very few things worth doing will come easily.

Incarnational leaders can find joy in their struggles. I am not talking about the joy of winning championships or starting some award-winning social service project. I am referring to finding joy in God throughout the journey and not just in the victory—in fact, finding joy in the journey when the victory never comes, when the program fails, or when your neighbor trudges back home unaffected by your carefully-chosen words of encouragement. There is not always a lot of surface level happiness in the daily grind of engaging an urban poor community for transformation, but when we seek God and trust his presence in it, there is a deep underlying joy.

A theology of suffering and struggle is important for all Christians, but the intensity of suffering in urban poor communities makes this theology all the more pressing. All Christians experience times when trusting God is the only thing they can do. These times simply seem to happen more often in the urban poor context.

Pause and Reflect:

1. When have you seen God show up in the midst of suffering?
2. How do you respond to the suffering of others? How do you respond to your own?
3. What external supports or internal attitudes have helped you to persevere in the midst of intense struggle?

Signs of Hope

Seeing God in everything also means that we are able to see the good within urban poor communities. Even in the midst of the most desperate situations, there are always signs of hope. Making a point of noticing the positive things that are happening can keep us from getting discouraged. During our prayer meetings, we have a time for expressing praises to God. Every once in a while, someone will simply praise God for another day of life. We can always praise God for life, and that we have been given another day to work toward the Kingdom.

Seeing the good also helps us to value and contribute to our communities. There are many aspects of urban poor life that are exemplary. The radical generosity of the urban poor toward each other has humbled and transformed my own ideas about community. We cannot undercut what God is already doing in our communities by refusing to acknowledge and build upon it.

There are signs of hope in transformed lives. The first baptismal service of BBCF was a joyful time of celebration. Six young men were baptized that day, and each of them shared how they came to know Jesus during the service. All of those who shared were in tears as they testified how God transformed their lives. Tears of joy were followed by laughter as the church family splashed and played in the swimming pool we rented for the baptism service. Since our first baptism service, many others have also come to know Jesus. In the midst of everything that is going wrong, we must acknowledge the powerful ways that God is moving.

Knowing the history of the community can help you to see how God has been at work over time. This has been helpful for us in Botocan, as the area has improved greatly over the years. A few decades ago, Botocan was plagued by violence. Today, it is a relatively safe place to live. Our personal incarnational ministry in Botocan is just a part of the transformation journey that has begun in the community. We acknowledge and celebrate the communal nature of God's work, embracing signs of hope from other ministries, from local politics, and from the daily lives of our neighbors.

Our transformative journey along the dirt and concrete alleyways continues. Our relationship with God has grown and stretched. We are able to see truths in Scripture we would have been blind to if it were not for our experience of living among the urban poor. As the transformation continues, Botocan springs to life like the hearty plants that sprout through the cracks in the concrete. These tiny green leaves announce the presence of life and give us hope as we continue on the journey of incarnational ministry among the urban poor.

Pause and Reflect:

1. What has your community shown you about God?
2. What do you love about your community? What do the local residents say they value most?
3. Share one transformation story from your community.

Conclusion

God is at work in the community. Remembering this is ultimately the only thing that sustains our ministry. Because we know that God is here, we are excited to be here, alongside him and alongside the poor—through persistent suffering and through signs of transformation.

ACKNOWLEDGMENTS

I am greatly indebted to all of those who contributed to this project. Thank you, Lord Jesus, for providing the ultimate example of incarnational leadership. Thank you to my wife, Ema, and our sons, Zach and Ezra, who allowed me to work countless hours on this project. I could not have completed it without your love and support. Thank you to all of those who set aside time from their busy schedules to meet with me for interviews. Thank you to my church family at Botocan Bible Christian Fellowship. Your faith has been much of the inspiration behind this project.

I feel the need to thank many of you by name, knowing that someone will be left out as I do so. Thank you to the Servant Partners domestic interns who read and commented on the early drafts of this book: Ben and Emily Margolis, Alison Blume, Stacey Agbonze, David Kitani, Bonnie Gordon, Lisa Keller, Anna Gilbreth, Erika Sutton, Kayla Morgan, Heather McClimans, Chelsea Tokuno, and Justin Liu. Thank you to everyone who served as editors and gave suggestions on content. Thank you to Randy White, Kevin Blue, Robert Linthicum, Elliot Ling, Daniel Taylor, Daniel Groot, Lisa Engdahl, Kristina and Aaron Whiting, Kristen Leber, Jerry Hogshead, Steve and Monica Mehaffey, Liz Heim, Krista-Dawn and Joel Kimsey, Andy Singleterry, Sarah Lane, Suzy Triplett, Sarah Ryer, Sara Smith, Joyce Chia-Hsin Lin, Jonathan Chang, Justine Wang, James Yu, Katie Gard, and Mark Walker. Thank you to Elizabeth Rhea and Bree Hsieh for your wonderful work on this second rendition of the text. It has been a joy to have each of you along for the ride.

APPENDIX A

WHY "INCARNATIONAL" MISSIONS?

By Derek Engdahl, General Director of Servant Partners
Excerpted from "Incarnational Missions: A Valid Model,"
Originally published as a blog post at ServantPartners.org

THE USE OF THE TERM *incarnation* to refer to a particular approach to ministry has recently fallen under the criticism of some sincere Christians.[72] One important critique is that it might be dangerous to try to "incarnate" with and among others, since it places the burden of witness on people and not the Spirit. It might seem as though incarnational witness depends on people looking at us instead of Christ. They argue that we should direct attention away from ourselves and toward Christ and the Spirit, who do the real work of breaking down the dividing wall of hostility between cultures and neighbors.

However, the term incarnational does not necessarily imply that the burden for witness falls upon ministers rather than the Holy Spirit. It is the Spirit who breaks down the dividing wall of hostility, but that doesn't mean that reconciliation happens magically. We still have to choose to love the other and the outcast, even to the point of sacrifice. Though there is a real risk that some might transfer credit to themselves, plenty of non-incarnational evangelists could fall into the same delusion. The obvious fact that we are not Jesus should be enough to dissuade people from believing that they or anyone else could reveal Jesus and the Father fully in their lives. We need to proclaim Jesus as someone infinitely better than and outside of ourselves, and tell people that they can be in relationship with him. We have to trust that the Holy Spirit alone converts hearts and transforms communities. None of this is in conflict with incarnational ministry.

Another critique is that there is only one incarnation and that if we try to imitate Jesus in this way, it cheapens what Christ has done by implying that it was not enough. But when we talk about incarnational ministry, we do not mean that we incarnate as Jesus did. Moving into a poor community, learning to speak the language, and seeking to walk alongside our neighbors is not the same as the Divine Word leaving the Father's side to become human and die on a cross so that we might be reconciled to him. But Jesus' incarnation is our model of love for the other. In the same way, when he calls us to take up our crosses and follow him, he does not intend for us to believe that our deaths will redeem humankind, but he does intend that our lives would be lived in imitation of his self-sacrifice. Our imitation of Christ's suffering does not deny the adequacy of Christ's unique atoning work on the cross, so it follows that imitating Jesus' incarnation does not deny its adequacy.

It is true that the followers of Jesus are never called to become "incarnate" in the Scripture, but the word is never used for Jesus either. It is a theological word, not a biblical one. That is not to say that the concept is not biblical. Jesus' incarnation is a very important theological truth deeply rooted in Scripture. But because the word is not used by any New Testament writer, I think we are free to see if the theological concept might apply to Jesus' followers in a specific and limited way. The question is whether the Bible calls us to imitate Jesus' incarnational model of ministry in the same way it calls us to imitate him in taking up our crosses. I believe it does.

An incarnational approach to ministry simply means seeking to leave what is known and comfortable in order to walk with those who are different so that we might expose them to Jesus and his Kingdom in their own context. This seems like what Jesus did himself, and called his followers to do as well. On a very practical level, this is an effective missiological strategy. The more we seek to live into another person's culture, the more we can shed and expand upon our own cultural understandings of the gospel and thereby allow it to manifest more fully and clearly. That's precisely what happened in the early church when the Gentiles started becoming followers of Jesus. Paul and Barnabas (through their experience in Antioch) and Peter (through his experience with Cornelius) were the first to realize, with the considerable help of the Holy Spirit, that the Jewish way they lived out the gospel did not need to be imposed on the new converts in a way that would burden them. In fact, if there was to be unity, some Jewish cultural practices would have to get dropped even by the Jews when they were with Gentile believers. Likewise, there were cultural practices that the Gentiles needed to give up for the sake of Jewish Christians as well. This is one of the positive tensions of an incarnational approach. Seeking to walk inside another culture should allow us to affirm the unique way that God is working in that context without imposing our own cultural interpretations.

Jesus told his disciples in John 13 that they would be recognized as his followers if they loved one another as he had loved them. Their love was to be part of their witness. Paul was on the same page. On numerous occasions, he talked about how his own suffering benefitted those to whom he was preaching. In 1 Thessalonians 4-7 he said, "For we know, brothers and sisters loved by

God, that he has chosen you because our gospel came to you not simply with words but also with power, with the Holy Spirit and deep conviction. You know how we lived among you for your sake. You became imitators of us and of the Lord, for you welcomed the message in the midst of severe suffering with the joy given by the Holy Spirit. And so you became a model to all the believers in Macedonia and Achaia." Here we see that proclamation and the work of the Holy Spirit are not in conflict with an incarnational approach. Paul talked about Jesus. The Spirit worked with power to confirm the message and convict the Thessalonians. Paul lived with them and modeled Christ to them and they in turn modeled Christ to others.

Many well-intentioned people want to say, "Don't look at me. Look at Jesus." Paul instead says, "Look at me and you will see the marks of the Jesus I have been telling you about." Maybe what is so frightening about an incarnational theology is not that it has a low view of Jesus or the Spirit, but that it has a higher view of what the church is supposed to be. If we understand our lives and churches as opportunities to manifest Christ and the Father, it is painfully obvious that we have fallen short. People are supposed to be able to see the Jesus we are united to, the Christ who now lives in us.

Two Servant Partners staff members, an Asian-American and a white South African, were hanging out with a few black residents of a squatter community in Johannesburg, South Africa. They were sharing food and drinks and enjoying each other's fellowship. Some other black residents walked by and commented aloud that they must be Servant Partners people, because who else would do such a thing? Non-black people do not usually come into poor black communities in South Africa to hang out with people, let alone live there with them. One would have hoped that the remark would have been that these people must be Christians, because who else would do such a thing? The fact is, though, that most Christians don't do such things, and those who made the comment knew this. Unfortunately, being Christian and living incarnationally are not often considered synonymous. But they are becoming a little more so as Christians continue to move into the world's cities to live as neighbors to the poor.

An incarnational approach to ministry allows us to be with people in their daily lives. It allows us to know them more fully and for them to know us. It affirms that we value them and their culture and that we desire to understand the struggles and joys that they experience. It also allows us to expose our flaws and failings so that we can declare that God's strength is made perfect in our weaknesses. It is a very concrete way we can love our neighbors as Jesus has loved us, and it permits us to live out the gospel and the Kingdom with them. If it is troubling for some to call this process "incarnation," then call it something else. The term is not important. The important thing is that we go and do likewise.

---

[72] See J. Todd Billings, "The Problem with Incarnational Ministry", *Christianity Today*, August 10, 2012, accessed December 1, 2015, *bit.ly/BillingsIncarnational* and also Tim Chester, "Why I Don't Believe in Incarnational Mission," *Tim Chester Blog,* July 19, 2008, accessed December 11, 2015, *bit.ly/timchesterincarnational.*

APPENDIX B

RESEARCH RESULTS

An excerpt from Chapter 6 of my doctoral dissertation
To read more, visit servantpartnerspress.org/ThrivingCity

In this chapter I will evaluate the research methodologies I used and present the findings and results of the research. I will reflect on the results of the two surveys, the interviews, and insights gleaned from both focus groups.

Evaluation of the Research Methodologies

Two surveys, multiple individual interviews, and two focus groups were the major research instruments used in this dissertation. The surveys provided information including what works best in regards to the approaches of living incarnationally, important keys for sustainability, and what areas new incarnational leaders need to focus on in their preparation. The limitation of both surveys was the difficulty of controlling variables.

This shortcoming was reflected in the surveys by the extensive use of "other" as an answer. The survey for current workers was mainly filled out by Servant Partners' staff, while the former staff of SERVANTS predominantly filled out the survey for former incarnational leaders. Comparisons between the two surveys are limited because it is unclear if differences stem from membership to Servant Partners or SERVANTS or between current and former incarnational leaders.

The interviews proved invaluable in verifying the survey results and providing keen insights on the practices and approaches of incarnational ministry. Notes were taken during the interviews, and they were recorded when it was deemed appropriate. When portions of the interviews were incorporated into the book, interviewees were asked to review the write-up for accuracy. Some of the interviews also helped expand the research for this project. For example, David, an incarnational leader with SERVANTS, described living meaningfully in an urban poor community as being in sync with the rhythms of the community.[73]

The focus groups were used to verify the survey results, as well as provide some best practices of incarnational ministry in an urban poor context. Both focus groups were recorded so they could be reviewed after the discussion. They revealed details as to how incarnational leaders take Sabbaths and live meaningfully in their communities.

Survey Results

In all, sixty-nine respondents submitted the survey for current incarnational leaders, and thirty-one respondents submitted the survey for former incarnational leaders.

A total of one hundred respondents submitted surveys for the research of this project.[74] The survey for current incarnational leaders revealed that 69 percent of the respondents preferred living slightly above the level of the average urban poor neighbor (*figure 1*). Those approaches that either limit time in the community or distinguish the incarnational leader from the community were given the lowest rankings. Those who marked these approaches were either living among the poor for twenty or more years, raising families, struggling with health concerns, or working in restricted countries.

FIGURE 1. *The approach that works well for current incarnational leaders*

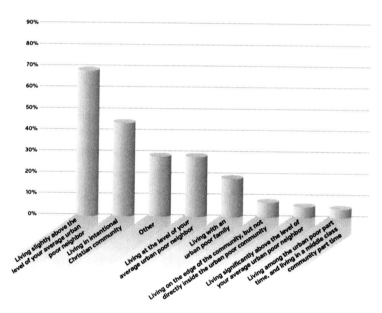

Note: Respondents were allowed to choose more than one answer, so percentages may not equal one hundred percent.

Not all incarnational leaders have experienced trauma while living among the urban poor. Twenty-eight percent stated that they had no major traumatic experiences.

The dominant traumatic experiences reported were property crime and a fire in the incarnational leaders' home or community. Life-threatening situations such as being stabbed, shot, or shot at were very rare. No one on either survey stated they were stabbed and only four on both surveys stated that they were shot or shot at. One of the four mentioned in a follow-up interview that she was in the vicinity of the shots but not directly shot at.

The experience of living in an urban poor community has predominantly been positive for current incarnational leaders' walk with God. Seventy-four percent stated they have grown closer to God during their time among the poor. In the midst of the pain of urban poor life, incarnational leaders are able to become sensitive to the work of God in their lives.

There are seasons to spiritual growth. Some respondents commented that their spiritual growth has gone through various seasons. One of the respondents on the survey for current incarnational leaders wrote that it "depends on the season whether I feel I am growing closer to God or feeling distant. But generally I believe it has been good for my spiritual journey."

Regular Sabbaths were the most life-giving spiritual discipline in both surveys. They are considered life-giving by 86 percent of current workers and 68 percent of former workers (*figure 2*).

FIGURE 2. *Life-giving spiritual disciplines for current incarnational leaders*

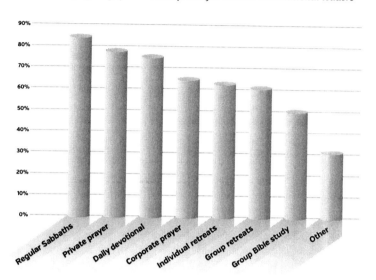

Note: Respondents were allowed to choose more than one answer, so percentages may not equal one hundred percent.

The main keys for sustainable incarnational ministry were a sense of calling (87 percent), disciplines (85 percent), and a healthy lifestyle (78 percent) (*figure 3*).

Spiritual disciplines were also cited as something that could have better prepared leaders for their ministries (61 percent for current workers, and 46 percent for former workers). The significance of these results illustrate that incarnational leaders recognized the vital importance of spiritual disciplines.

FIGURE 3. *Keys for sustainability for current incarnational leaders*

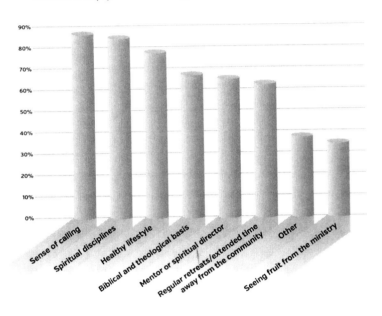

Note: Respondents were allowed to choose more than one answer, so percentages may not equal one hundred percent.

The survey of former workers revealed that while living among the urban poor is not the only or even dominant factor for people leaving, it does play a role (*figure 4*).

Incarnational leaders need support systems in place to ensure sustainability. Areas such as self-care, member care, health, and family issues all need to be addressed by incarnational leaders among the urban poor.

If given a chance to do it again, the major changes that former incarnational leaders would have made include taking better care of their health (35 percent), taking more time off (32 percent), and going on a different team (29 percent). Taking better care of one's health and taking more time off both fall under self-care and reveal that it is important for incarnational leaders to take care of their bodies in order to be more sustainable.

FIGURE 4. *Impact of incarnational living on the decision to leave*

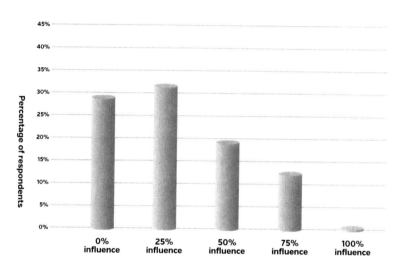

The survey for current incarnational leaders asked the open-ended question, "What advice do you have for someone who is new to incarnational ministry?" Several themes emerged from the responses. The range of focus was broad, so even those themes that were repeated multiple times did not include a large percentage of respondents. One of the dominant themes was spiritual disciplines and maintaining a strong relationship with God. Advice related to spiritual disciplines or growing closer to God was given by 26 percent of the respondents. The advice either referred directly to spiritual disciplines or named a specific discipline, such as prayer. Of the specific spiritual disciplines referred to, having a regular Sabbath or some kind of retreat was mentioned by 13 percent of the respondents. Current incarnational leaders stress the importance of having some kind of break from the chaos of the community and being able to disengage.

The importance of developing healthy relationships was another prominent theme. Issues related to relationships were mentioned by 15 percent of the respondents. The reason for this advice was the emotional health of the incarnational leader, as well as practical effectiveness in ministry. Having a mentor or spiritual director was another dominant theme. Eleven percent of the respondents gave the advice to have a mentor or spiritual director. The minor reoccurring themes that emerged were the advice to be a learner, be flexible, be patient, and love life.

Interview Results

A total of twenty-one interviews were conducted with a broad range of incarnational leaders including seniors who have lived among the poor for decades, young adults who have recently relocated, and parents.[75] Three interviews were with incarnational leaders who moved out of an urban poor community. These interviews revealed that while the realities of urban poor life played a role in the decision to leave, it was not the main reason. One married couple who moved out of an urban poor community stated, "We had a difficult time managing physically with much sickness and physical weakness, but we both agreed all along that physical illness and suffering in itself would not cause us to leave."[76] This experience was supported by the survey, which revealed that nobody left purely because of living incarnationally.

Four parents were interviewed. There was a wide variety of thoughts on the specific practices of parenting; however, interviews always focused on the themes of education, negative influences, and safety. These topics are what parents were most concerned about. Parents also recognized the positive aspects of raising their children among the urban poor. Kevin Blue, an incarnational leader in Los Angeles, recognized that raising his two boys in an urban poor community has "the possibility for greater a perspective on life."[77] The parents interviewed felt alone in this perspective and did not realize that other parents also recognized the potential benefits of raising children in an urban poor environment. Betty Sue Brewster shared the wise parenting advice that "children cannot decide what God's will is. There are seasons when, for the sake of the children, ministry will be adjusted. However, just because the child likes a certain place better is not a reason why that location should be chosen. The major piece is listening to the Lord."[78] Ultimately, incarnational leaders need faith that God is behind their decisions to minister incarnationally among the urban poor.

Robert Linthicum provided useful insights for engaging the community for transformation. He shared that "for every minute spent in action, a minute should be spent in reflection."[79] This insight stresses the importance of having the discipline of reflection and regular evaluations. The process of thinking about actions of engagement allows incarnational leaders to grow and more effectively work for the transformation of a community.

The interviews provided vital insights regarding the various approaches to incarnational ministry. Interviewing the former member of an intentional community helped me understand the importance of detailed planning before starting an intentional community in order to determine vision and the particulars of communal living (such as purchasing groceries and chores).[80] I was also able to interview two singles and one married couple whose approach to incarnational ministry was to live with an urban poor family. Their responses helped me understand the advantages and disadvantages of living with a family as well as important insights regarding what to look for when discerning a family to live with, such as to make sure that the family is financially and emotionally stable. It is also helpful for the family to have some awareness of cross-cultural differences.[81]

Focus Group Results

The focus group for the Internships Department had ten attendees. The internship staff discussed how the survey revealed individual spiritual disciplines were considered more life-giving than corporate disciplines. A consensus was reached that life-giving spiritual disciplines are individual with a corporate element such as having others to pray and debrief with.

When reflecting on keys to sustainability, the focus group observed there was no one all-important key to sustainability. There are a variety of factors that need to be in place. I noticed that "seeing fruit from the ministry" was stated as a key to sustainability for only 35 percent of the respondents. The focus group determined that incarnational leaders mentally know that fruit is not the most important part. On the other hand it is important to recognize that it is difficult to have years of ministry without seeing fruit.

While seeing fruit is not a major key to sustainability, incarnational leaders need to be able to deal with seasons of fruitlessness; thus a healthy theology of failure is vital to have hope and see the small successes.

The second focus group was held during Servant Partners' All Staff Conference and had seventeen attendees. This focus group reflected on life-giving Sabbaths. For many international incarnational leaders, a Sabbath meant spending the night outside the community. The focus group stressed flexibility and realized that as seasons of life change, the specifics of practicing a weekly Sabbath will also change.

The focus group noted the importance of calling as a key to sustainability. We discussed ways to remember one's calling such as having regular reflection times both individually and corporately. Accountability was an important factor to help keep the call fresh.

Time was also spent discussing life-giving ways of living meaningfully in an urban poor community. There was an emphasis on building friendships with neighbors. Relationships were built through activities such as spending personal time in the community and opening up one's home for neighbors to visit.

Appreciative Inquiry influenced the focus groups since the discussions focused on what was life-giving rather than on where participants have struggled. This approach was well received as both groups engaged in lively discussions regarding what worked. It encouraged participants to share the important sustainability factors in their ministry.

---

[73] Interview with David Cross.

[74] See Appendix E of my dissertation for the full Survey Results for Current Incarnational Leaders and Appendix F for the full Survey Results for Former Incarnational Leaders.

[75] The twenty-one interviews listed do not include the six interviews that were conducted with Botocan residents nor does it include follow-up communication for clarification regarding survey responses.

[76] Interview with "Ryan," July 28, 2011. Charlottesville, VA.

[77] Interview with Kevin Blue, August 6, 2011. Indian Wells, CA.

[78] Interview with Betty Sue Brewster, August 8, 2011. Indian Wells, CA.

[79] Interview with Robert Linthicum.

[80] Interview with "John."

[81] Interview with Jen Chi Lee, August 9, 2011. Indian Wells, CA.

APPENDIX C

INCARNATIONAL SENDING ORGANIZATIONS

These are some of the many organizations that have a history of ministering incarnationally among the urban poor. Most offer internship opportunities.

InnerCHANGE
www.innerchange.org

InterVarsity Christian Fellowship
www.InterVarsity.org

Servant Partners*
www.ServantPartners.org

Servants to Asia's Urban Poor (SERVANTS)
www.servantsasia.org

Urban Neighbors of Hope (UNOH)
www.unoh.org

Word Made Flesh
www.wordmadeflesh.org

---

* T. Aaron Smith's sending organization

GLOSSARY OF TERMS AND LOCATIONS

ASIAN THEOLOGICAL SEMINARY (ATS). An evangelical seminary in Manila, Philippines.

BALIC-BALIC. A squatter community established along a railroad track in Manila, Philippines. My first home among the urban poor. It was destroyed by the government in 2008.

BALIC-BALIC COMMUNITY CHURCH (BBCC). The church that invited me into Balic-Balic when I was a student. I was a pastor of this church for one year.

BOTOCAN. A squatter community in Metro Manila, Philippines. My current home.

BOTOCAN BIBLE CHRISTIAN FELLOWSHIP (BBCF). A church that my wife and I helped to plant with local Christians in Botocan.

CHURCH PLANTING. Organizing Christians in a community to begin meeting as a congregation, establishing an identity, leadership structures, and activities.

COMMUNITY-BASED INCARNATIONAL MINISTRY. Living meaningfully in a community and engaging that community for transformation in Christ.

CONTEXTUALIZATION. Customizing teaching, programming, and interactions to fit the community.

FAITH GOSPEL COMMUNITY (FGC). A sister church in Botocan.

IDENTIFICATION. The mindset of becoming one with the poor, being able to relate to their poverty, and struggling with them in solidarity.

INCARNATIONAL LEADER. One who lives meaningfully in a community and engages his or her community for transformation.

INCARNATIONAL MINISTRY. Meaningful presence and engagement for transformation.

INTEGRAL MISSION. The natural blending of evangelism and social action, including community organizing and other methods of engagement.

INTENTIONAL COMMUNITY. A group of Christians living together in the same house for the purpose of ministry.

JEEPNEY. A common form of public transportation in Manila, designed after World War II troop transport vehicles.

MAJORITY WORLD. Describes regions outside of the developed west. It replaces the term *third world*, which might imply that these places are less important or that they are the exception, rather than the rule.

NEW FRIARS. A specific movement of modern incarnational leaders who identify with the traditional Christian role of friar.

SQUATTER. A person or community that resides on land which was not purchased through official deeds and titles, putting them at risk for eviction and demolition.

TRANSFORMATION. I use this word to describe when a society or neighborhood begins to reflect the Kingdom, rather than a change of internal feeling in an individual.

TAGALOG. The most common Filipino language used in Manila.

TRICYCLE. A motorcycle with a sidecar for transporting passengers.

URBAN POOR COMMUNITIES. Densely packed and under-resourced neighborhoods near urban centers whose residents are vulnerable to oppression and exploitation. This term is the most neutral, while slang terms like slum, ghetto, and hood add other connotations to the concept.

SELECTED BIBLIOGRAPHY

Recommended follow-up reading is indicated in bold.

Bakke, Ray. *A Theology as Big as the City*. Downers Grove, IL: InterVarsity Press, 1997.

Bakke, Ray, and Jim Hart. *The Urban Christian: Effective Ministry in Today's Urban World*. Downers Grove, IL: InterVarsity Press, 1987.

Bessenecker, Scott. *The New Friars: The Emerging Movement Serving the World's Poor*. Downers Grove, IL: InterVarsity Press, 2006.

_____, ed. *Living Mission: The Vision and Voices of New Friars*. Downers Grove, IL: InterVarsity Press, 2010.

Blue, Kevin. *Practical Justice: Living Off-Center in a Self-Centered World*. Downers Grove, IL: InterVarsity Press, 2006.

Bright, John. *Jeremiah*. Garden City: Doubleday, 1965.

Brueggemann, Walter. *A Commentary on Jeremiah: Exile and Homecoming*. Grand Rapids: Eerdmans, 1998.

Chester, Tim. "Why I Don't Believe in Incarnational Mission," *Tim Chester Blog*, July 19, 2008, *bit.ly/timchesterincarnational* (accessed December 11, 2015).

Claerbaut, David. *Urban Ministry in a New Millennium*. 2d ed. Waynesboro, GA: Authentic Media, 2005.

Costas, Orlando E. *Christ Outside the Gate: Mission Beyond Christendom*. Maryknoll, NY: Orbis Books, 1984.

Craig, Jenni M. *Servants among the Poor*. Manila: OMF Literature, 1998.

Daes, David, ed. *Caring for the Least of These: Serving Christ among the Poor*. Scottdale, PA: Herald Press, 1992.

Douglas, J. D. et al. *New Bible Dictionary*. Downers Grove, IL: InterVarsity Press, 1993.

Duncan, Michael. *Costly Mission: Following Christ into the Slums*. Monrovia, CA: MARC, 1996.

_____. *The Incarnational Approach*. Christchurch: SERVANTS, 1991.

Gornik, Mark. *To Live in Peace: Biblical Faith and the Changing Inner City*. Grand Rapids: Eerdmans, 2002.

Greenway, Roger S. *Discipling the City: A Comprehensive Approach to Urban Mission*. 2d ed. Grand Rapids: Baker, 1992.

Greenway, Roger S., and Timothy M. Monsma. *Cities: Missions' New Frontier*. 2d ed. Grand Rapids: Baker, 2000.

Grigg, Viv. *Companion to the Poor: Christ in the Urban Slums*. 3d ed. Waynesboro, GA: Authentic Media, 2004.

_____. *Cry of the Urban Poor: Reaching the Slums of Today's Mega-Cities*. 2d ed. Waynesboro, GA: Authentic Media, 2005.

_____. *A Strategy to Reach the Urban Poor of the Third World's Great Cities*. Pasadena, CA: SERVANTS among the Poor, 1987.

Hayes, John B. *Sub-Merge: Living Deep in a Shallow World*. Ventura, CA: Regal, 2006.

Hiebert, Paul G., and Eloise Hiebert Meneses. *Incarnational Ministry: Planting Churches in Band, Tribal, Peasant, and Urban Societies*. Grand Rapids: Baker, 1995.

Hill, Harriet. "Incarnational Ministry: A Critical Examination." *Evangelical Missions Quarterly* 26:2 (1990): 196-201.

Jack, Kristin, ed. *The Sound of Worlds Colliding: Stories of Radical Discipleship from Servants to Asia's Urban Poor*. Phnom Penh, Cambodia: Hawaii Printing House, 2009.

Kramer, Mark. *Dispossessed: Life in Our World's Urban Slums*. Maryknoll, NY: Orbis Books, 2006.

Lapierre, Dominique. *The City of Joy*. New York: Warner Books, 1992.

Linthicum, Robert C. *Building a People of Power: Equipping Churches to Transform Their Communities*. Waynesboro, GA: Authentic Media, 2006.

Lupton, Robert D. *Renewing the City: Reflections on Community Development and Urban Renewal*. Downers Grove, IL: InterVarsity Press, 2005.

Manalili, Angelito G. *Community Organizing for People's Empowerment*. Manila: Kapatiran-Kaunlaran Foundation, 1990.

Milne, Bruce. *The Message of John: Here Is Your King! The Bible Speaks Today*. Leicester, England: Inter-Varsity Press, 1993.

Neuwirth, Robert. *Shadow Cities: A Billion Squatters, a New Urban World*. New York: Routledge, Taylor & Francis, 2006.

Perkins, John. *With Justice for All*. Ventura, CA: Regal, 1982.

Perkins, John, and Jo Kadlecek. *Resurrecting Hope*. Ventura, CA: Regal, 1995.

Powell, Kara, Jude Tiersma Watson, and Cynthia Eriksson. "Stress in the City: A New Study of Youth Workers." Fuller Youth Institute. *bit.ly/fyi-stressinthecity* (accessed October 13, 2010).

Samuel, Vinay, and Chris Sugden. "Agenda for Missions in the Eighties and Nineties: A Discussion Starter." In *New Frontiers in Mission*. Edited by Patrick Sookhdeo. Exeter, UK: Paternoster Press, 1987.

Smith, Brad. *City Signals: Principles and Practices for Ministering in Today's Global Communities*. Birmingham, AL: New Hope Publishing, 2008.

Smith, T. Aaron. "The Bible and Urban Poverty: Community Bible Interpretation among the Urban Poor in Manila." *Journal of Asian Mission* 12:2 (2010): 171-187.

_____. "Living among the Urban Poor: The Practices and Approaches of Incarnational Ministry." DMin diss., Bakke Graduate University, 2012.

Thompson, J. A. *The Book of Jeremiah*. NICOT. Grand Rapids: Eerdmans, 1980.

Tiersma, Jude. "What Does It Mean to Be Incarnational When We Are Not the Messiah?" In *God So Loves the City: Seeking a Theology for Urban Mission*, edited by Charles Van Engen and Jude Tiersma. Monrovia, CA: MARC, 1994.

White, Randy. *Encounter God in the City: Onramps to Personal and Community Transformation*. Downers Grove, IL: InterVarsity Press, 2006.

Wilkerson, David, John Sherrill, and Elizabeth Sherrill. *The Cross and the Switchblade*. Old Tappan, NJ: Chosen Books, 1963.

INDEX OF INTERVIEWS

Interviews that were directly quoted or paraphrased in this book are indicated with their page numbers. Other interviews contributed to my understanding of trends and may have been quoted in my dissertation.

Interviews with Incarnational Leaders

Ling, Elliot. August 16, 2011. Los Angeles, CA. (160)

Linthicum, Robert. August 9, 2011. Indian Wells, CA. (166, 197)

Mathieson, Dorothy. August 10, 2011. Indian Wells, CA.

Palmer, Dave. July 28, 2011. Charlottesville, VA. (57)

Palmer, Joshua. October 18, 2011. Tanay, Philippines.

"Ryan" (Anonymous). July 28, 2011. Charlottesville, VA. (196)

Taylor, Daniel. August 12, 2011. Indian Wells, CA.

Withers, Ashley. August 4, 2011. e-mail. (105)

Interviews with Community Members in Botocan

Amplayohan, Jiovane. July 3, 2011. Quezon City, Philippines. (47)

Gaupo, Amy. July 2, 2011. Quezon City, Philippines.

Janga, Alire. July 2, 2011. Quezon City, Philippines.

Jenga, Reymon. July 4, 2011. Quezon City, Philippines.

Lana, Angelica. July 2, 2011. Quezon City, Philippines.

Limlengco, Ma. Gracita. July 3, 2011. Quezon City, Philippines.

ABOUT THE AUTHOR

T. Aaron Smith leads the Servant Partners team in Manila, Philippines, where he serves as a founding leader of Botocan Bible Christian Fellowship. He also directs the Transformational Urban Leadership program at Asian Theological Seminary in Manila, and is the lead instructor in Servant Partners' Global Urban Training School, Foundations. He earned a Master's of Divinity from Asian Theological Seminary, and a Doctor of Ministry from Bakke Graduate University in Seattle, Washington. Aaron and his wife, Ema, and their sons, Zach and Ezra, continue to live and serve among the urban poor.

SERVANT PARTNERS PRESS

SERVANT PARTNERS PRESS

Proclaiming God's Presence among the Urban Poor

Servant Partners Press is dedicated to supporting the growing movement of people who are called to live and work alongside the urban poor. We publish theological reflections, narratives, and training materials that speak to God's transforming power in the inner cities and slums of our world.

To learn more about Servant Partners Press or to purchase books, visit us at *ServantPartnersPress.org.*

CPSIA information can be obtained
at www.ICGtesting.com
Printed in the USA
FFOW03n1323210517
35728FF